Benchmarking Identifiable Intangibles and Their Useful Lives in Business Combinations

SECOND EDITION

BVR
What It's Worth
1000 SW Broadway, Suite 1200, Portland OR 97205
(503) 291-7963 • www.bvresources.com

BVR
What It's Worth

Editor: Adam Manson

Publisher: Sarah Andersen

Managing Editor: Janice Prescott

Chair and CEO: David Foster

President: Lucretia Lyons

Vice President of Sales: Lexie Gross

Customer Service Manager: Retta Dodge

ISBN: 978-1-62150-056-8

Library of Congress Control Number: 2015951284

Table of Contents

Introduction

The value of an intangible asset is typically a function of the future economic income that is expected to be derived from the ownership or operation of that intangible asset during its expected remaining useful life (RUL). All three of the generally accepted intangible asset valuation approaches (i.e., income approach, market approach, and cost approach) depend, to varying degrees, on the expected RUL of the subject intangible asset.

Traditionally, IP values have been underreported in financial statements, due mainly to two factors that stem from generally accepted accounting principles (GAAP):

- Internally grown intangible assets are neither capitalized nor reported on the balance sheet; rather, their historical costs (design, prosecute and maintain, promote, defend, etc.) are expensed as spent; and
- A vague/mysterious/opaque goodwill category has been utilized to capture the all-encompassing excess of the purchase price over book value paid in mergers and acquisitions.

In 2001, the Financial Accounting Standards Board (FASB) issued statements 141 (now ASC 805) and 142 to reform that practice. The changes created a uniform procedure whereby the acquiring entity in a business combination must perform a purchase price allocation (PPA) that matches the purchase price to asset values of the acquired company, including, importantly, intangible assets. Intangibles based on contracts and legal rights are distinguished from general goodwill, which remains a residual value.

What intangibles are valuation analysts isolating and CFOs reporting in PPAs? What remaining useful lives are they assigning? Are there industry nuances? Heretofore, analysts have been on their own in estimating remaining useful lives, without significant benchmarks. Auditors have been at a similar loss, as have CFOs.

Pamela Garland, in "Estimating IP Remaining Useful Life," a 2004 *Willamette Insights* article, outlined the importance of remaining useful lives of intangibles:

When a cost approach method is used, RUL should be considered in the estimation of obsolescence. When an income approach method is performed, RUL should be considered in determining the term of the income projection period. When a market approach method is used, RUL is a factor (1) in assessing the comparability of the market transactions to the subject property and (2) in estimating any adjustments to make the guideline sale/license transactions more comparative to the subject property.

Willamette Management Associates explained the difference between a business valuation and valuation of intangible assets in detail at a National Association of Certified Valuation Analysts (NACVA) conference.

Exhibit 1 highlights the importance of a remaining useful life analysis in valuation of intangible assets.

Exhibit 1. Importance of Remaining Useful Life Analysis in Valuation of Intangible Assets

Analysis variables	Intangible asset valuation	Business valuation
Operating income	That portion attributable to asset	All
Life	Limited remaining useful life (RUL)	Usually in perpetuity
Discount rate	Higher	Lower
Obsolescence	Affects RUL	Business adapts
"Highest and best use"	Requires analysis	Management usually knows
Approaches	Income, market, cost	Income, market, asset-based
Legal rights	Several ownership interests	Fee simple interest

The purpose of the research in this publication is not to provide complete coverage of intangible property valuation methodologies and theory. Rather, it is a compilation of useful, reported data, particularly on remaining useful lives of intangible assets, as well as their value relative to the total amount of intangible assets and to the business's selling price, as reflected in over 6,000 purchase price allocations, gleaned from the databases available at Business Valuation Resources, LLC.[1] That being said, this work provides other useful data such as:

1. *Valuing noncompete agreements.* Analysts many times feel they have to work in a vacuum when valuing noncompetes. It is important to benchmark against what others are finding in similar industries and with similar deal sizes. Data in this volume provide such benchmarks.

2. *Dominance of intangible assets.* Scientific, financial, and lay press articles repeatedly suggest the ratio of intangible assets to total assets is large and growing. This concept buttresses the idea that these assets need to be managed, that growth and sustainability are dependent upon the attention paid to intangibles. To our knowledge, no statistical compilation derived directly from fair value valuations of intangibles and total assets has ever been compiled to support these statistical claims with hard data—until now. The ratio of intangible assets to total assets defined by this detailed study of purchase price allocations is 72%.

1. Data analyzed for this study are contained in the *Public Stats* and *Pratt's Stats* databases, which are available at www.bvresources.com.

3. *Spotlight on amortization tendencies.* Benchmarking "living" data for intangibles also has the side benefit, primarily for investors, of spotlighting who is stringing out amortization, perhaps to inflate current income, and who is taking more rapid appreciation, perhaps to minimize taxes.

Who will use this publication?

1. Valuation analysts will use this work to benchmark what intangibles are being discovered, categorized, and valued in specific industries, as well as to provide remaining useful life guidance, noncompete agreement benchmarks, and benchmarks as to industry.

2. Auditors want to know what others are doing.

3. CFOs take on the Sarbanes-Oxley responsibility when purchase price allocation valuations are reported and require a close look at amortization rationales.

4. Investors will see benchmark data they have never seen before, gleaned from public filings, to compare to a target company's intangible property strength, amortization strategies, and composition of goodwill.

How to use this guide. There are three ways into this study. The first is by reviewing the various intangibles, wherein descriptions of valuation approaches are coupled with checklists of factors to consider. Here, readers get a good feel for the nature of the intangibles before proceeding to the statistical data on valuations and remaining useful lives (RULs).

The second is to go directly to Chapter 9 for data slices organized by intangible.

The third approach is to go directly to Chapter 10 for data slices showing how intangibles valued in business combinations are treated by industry.

On page 9 is a brief explanation of purchase price allocations, the source of data for this study. Exhibit 2 on page 10 is a graphic representation of how to determine identifiable intangible assets in PPAs. On page 11 begins a long list of FASB-identifiable intangible asset categories. (Readers who wish to see what is being identified by industry can move directly to industry data slices in the back of the study.)

Chapter 1. Purchase Price Allocations: Definitions and Authority

Prior to June 2001, financial accounting for intangible assets in business combinations followed APB Opinions 16 and 17, issued in 1970, which allowed for using the pooling of interests method and called for any goodwill recorded following an acquisition to be amortized over a period not to exceed 40 years, respectively. (Most companies adopted the 40-year maximum as the useful life in computing amortization to maximize periodic earnings.) Goodwill was a parking place for intangible assets.

Pooling of interests allowed companies to add the book value of acquired net assets to their balance sheet. In FAS 141, concluding that all business combinations (other than joint ventures) are, in effect, acquisitions and that one of the combining entities will be a surviving entity, the Financial Accounting Standards Board (FASB or Board) determined that, after June 30, 2001, the purchase method of accounting for business combinations will be the only permitted method (for for-profit companies only, and not including asset exchanges or transfers between entities under common control), and fair value will be the uniform standard of value to be used in valuing the assets of the acquired entity. In other words, the FASB required allocation of the total consideration in an acquisition, regardless of the manner of disposition of that consideration, to individual assets acquired, including financial assets, tangible assets, and intangible assets based on their fair values. And, after the issuance of FAS 142, goodwill was to be treated as a nonamortizable intangible asset requiring minimally annual review for possible impairment.

FAS 141 recognized that amortizable intangible assets are distinct from goodwill and established that when the total value of goodwill and other intangible assets is a significant portion of the total assets acquired, as it now is in most business combinations, more information regarding the distinct valuations of those intangibles needs to be determined and revealed.

The FASB concluded that an intangible asset should be recognized apart from goodwill if either: (1) control over the future economic benefits of the asset results from contractual or other legal rights (the contractual-legal criterion); or (2) the intangible asset is capable of being separated or divided and sold, transferred, licensed, rented, or exchanged (either separately or as part of a group of assets) (the separability criterion, or SLERT).

Currently analysts are encouraged to apply SLERT criteria (see Exhibit 2) to the determination of whether an intangible asset should be recognized separately from goodwill. Is the asset separable, licensable, exchangeable, rentable, or transferable?

Exhibit 2. Identification of Intangibles for Inclusion in Purchase Price Allocations

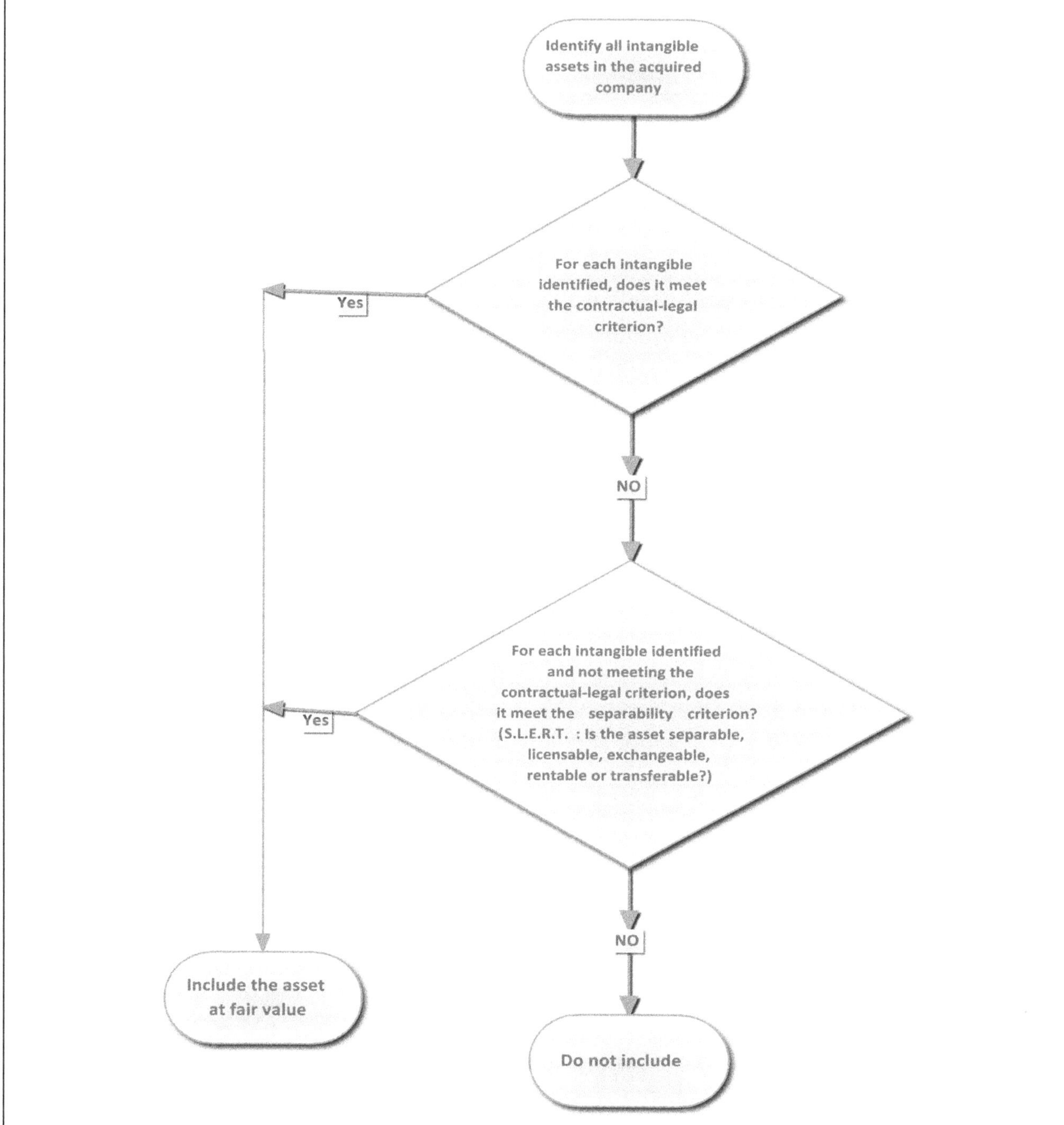

The FASB felt that it should not limit intangible assets that meet the separability criterion to only those that are exchanged in observable transactions, concluding that the intent to sell or otherwise exchange the asset is not the relevant factor to distinguish an intangible asset from goodwill; rather, it is the asset's *capability* of being separated from the entity and exchanged for something else of value.

The standard also listed these categories or classes of intangible assets for analysts performing PPAs:

Marketing intangibles[2]

Marketing-related intangible assets are those assets used in the marketing or promotion of products or services and/or in the establishment of a brand. Note: The terms "brand" and "brand name" often are used as synonyms for trademarks and trade names. The FASB did not preclude an entity from recognizing a brand as a single marketing-related intangible asset representing a group of complementary intangible assets if the assets that make up that group have similar useful lives.

- Trademarks;
- Trade names;
- Service marks, collective marks, and certification marks;
- Trade dress;
- Trade secrets, such as secret formulas, processes, and recipes;
- Newspaper mastheads;
- Noncompete agreements; and
- Internet domain names.

Customer intangibles

- Customer lists;
- Order backlog;
- Customer contracts and related customer relationships; and
- Noncontractual customer relationships.

Artistic intangibles

- Plays, operas, and ballets;
- Books, magazines, newspapers, and other literary works;
- Musical works such as compositions, song lyrics, and advertising jingles;
- Pictures and photographs; and
- Video and audiovisual material, including motion pictures, music videos, and television programs.

2 From *Valuing Intangibles: Surviving FASB 141 & 142 Assignments,* Institute of Business Appraisers Class #1035 , Pittsburgh, July 9, 2007.

Contract-based intangibles

- Licensing, royalty, and standstill agreements;
- Advertising, construction, management, and service or supply contracts;
- Lease agreements;
- Construction permits;
- Franchise agreements;
- Operating and broadcast rights;
- Use rights such as drilling, water, air, mineral, timber cutting, and route authorities;
- Servicing contracts such as mortgage servicing contracts; and
- Employment contracts.

Technology-based intangibles

- Patented technology;
- Computer software and mask works;
- Unpatented technology;
- Databases, including title plants; and
- Trade secrets, such as secret formulas, processes, and recipes.

FAS 141 defined fair value as the amount for which an asset could be purchased or sold in a current transaction between willing parties (parties not in a forced sale situation). The approaches used to value the intangibles are familiar to valuators worldwide:

1. The cost approach uses the cost of reproduction or replacement of the asset;
2. The market approach uses similar arm's-length agreements (purchase and sale agreements and licenses) as comparables; and
3. The income approach estimates asset value based on the present value of an assumed income stream (remaining useful life of the asset is a critical element).

As with business valuations in general, one or more of the approaches may be appropriate for the valuation of an intangible asset in a PPA.

Chapter 2. Technology

Valuators are commonly asked to find and measure technology assets. These could be developed technology, software, databases, etc. Patented or not, if it's proprietary, it probably adds value to the acquired entity.

The Statement of Financial Accounting Standards #141 categorizes technology assets thus:

a. Patented technology;

b. Computer software and mask works;

c. Unpatented technology;

d. Databases, including title plants; and

e. Trade secrets, such as secret formulas, processes, and recipes. (Trade secrets are covered in Chapter 3.)

A. PATENTED TECHNOLOGY

Valuators need to determine the legal life of any existing patents, but a complete analysis of the relevance and staying power of the technology behind the patent needs to be performed to determine useful life. Who are the competitors? How frequently does the technology reinvent itself? What is the history of the technology in question?

For this reason, purchase price allocations seldom refer to patents, choosing rather to value "technology" as an intangible, most generally divided into acquired technology and core or developed technology.

Fernando Torres, writing in BVR's *IP Management and Valuation* in January 2012, described the fundamental principles of patent valuation:

1. A patent is only the temporary right to exclude others from a specific market delimited by a written description of an innovation; it has no intrinsic value outside the value of a business; it does not represent the right to practice an invention or entitlement to a royalty income stream.

Several factors determine the potential economic value of the opportunity the patent represents. For example, if an inventor is issued a patent on an innovation that he or she cannot implement directly and no one else needs such invention to operate their business and satisfy actual consumer demands, then no actual market segment exists for the invention. What's more, that patent is not simply worthless; it actually represents a net cost to the patent holder in covering drafting, drawings, filing fees, and other prosecution costs that, realistically, are no less than $1,500 and could be as high as 10 times that amount.

By contrast, when there is market demand for, say, an accessory that props up touchscreen smartphones because: (1) a large number of such phones are in use; (2) the phones must be held at an angle for comfortable viewing of videos; (3) the cost of manufacturing the accessory is low relative to the phone at the appropriate volume levels; and (4) demand exists for accessories that enhance the functionality of the phones. In this case, the value of this limited accessory business would be proportional to the net profits of the venture. More specifically, a patent for that invention would likely have economic value because the patent holder can exclude others from making, importing, using, offering for sale, or selling that invention throughout the U.S. and sell the product at, or up to, a monopoly price—the price at which the seller maximizes net profits beyond the market compensation of the capital and other resources employed. Typically, this price would be greater than the competitive price for the product, i.e., the price at which this seller would be operating at the general profitability level. Conceptually, the patent-holding seller would maximize profits at a lower production level that is more than proportionately compensated by a higher price.

Referring back to the hypothetical phone accessory business, insofar as such a business can have value, a patent on the device would have economic value by excluding competitors. The value of that patent is related to, but different from, the value of the underlying business (and usually smaller if the business is profitable in a competitive environment). Consequently, an initial conclusion based on this principle is that the question for the patent holder is not "what is my patent worth?" Rather, it would be closer to "what is the value of the underlying business, and how much can a patent contribute to that business value?"

2. A patent's use is a key arbiter of its value. In practice, patents can have several uses, and each alternative brings characteristics and contextual parameters that affect economic value. Once a patent holder is in possession of an issued patent, it can be put to economic use in at least one of the following ways:

a. *Internal.* The patent holder may make use of the patent internally in an existing business (or firm). The patent may cover a specific aspect or an improvement of the manufacturing process used in the firm or it might cover a specific feature of a product. In addition, the patent could be a method patent and claim a specific mode of operating the business—or implementing a procedure in software, for example. Internal users typically supplement new patents with existing resources, trade secrets, and knowledge assets to put them in practical use. For example, Apple Inc. regularly obtains patents on its own future product designs or for product features that it plans to incorporate into its products.

b. *Licensing.* The patent holder may focus on licensing the patent to third parties, with the goal of developing a royalty income stream by relying on the licensees to bring together any additional resources to practice the claimed invention. IBM has been granted more patents than any other U.S. company during each year since 1993. It maintains a broad portfolio of patents in the computer industry, specializing in display, storage, network computing, and software. Yet IBM does not manufacture products in these areas anymore; it licenses its technologies to third parties that engage in manufacturing. One technique increasingly used to establish a licensing program has been the threat of litigation. This strategy has been the choice for companies described as nonpracticing entities or, less euphemistically, patent trolls.

c. *Blocking.* The patent holder might not use the process, manufacture a product, or license third parties but rather hold on to it to block competitors from developing specific products or benefiting from some innovations. Typically, this use is not publicized, for obvious reasons. Take the example of a car manufacturer that had been the first to patent fuel injectors but did not use them in its vehicles nor license them. The competition would have to continue using carburetor-based engines as long as the threat of patent infringement was perceived as real, and the patent-holding car company could buy a head start in developing a better fuel injection system for the future, thus staying two steps ahead of the competition.

d. *Mixed licensing.* A patentee could have a patent on, for example, a way of compressing and decompressing video to facilitate its transmission over the Internet. The main way in which the patentee can profit from this is if the whole industry uses it and, specifically, if the patent holder licenses everyone to use it (even at very low royalties) along with the patentee's own internal use.

e. *Cross-licensing.* In many industries that are host to active patenting, such as telecommunications or pharmaceutical research, patent holders often use patents as bartering pieces to cancel out the threat of infringement litigation from competitors. They do this by licensing some of their patents to the holders of patents they need to compete or patents they are likely to be found infringing. A case in point is a recent agreement whereby Intel Corp. (the company famous for its microprocessors) received a license to Nvidia Corp.'s patents, while Nvidia (the company famous for its graphics processors) got a license to some of Intel's patents, thus resolving outstanding litigation between them. As part of the deal, Intel will pay Nvidia $1.5 billion in royalties over five years.

f. *Sleeping or submarine patents.* Sometimes, patent holders do not apply, license, cross-license, or litigate their patents. Instead, they wait until a suitable target appears or patents are simply shelved (sometimes forgotten) as a consequence of an overly active patenting drive or bad management.

The value principles examined here aim to provide, as a starting point, questions that must be posed and answered before a meaningful assessment of patent value is undertaken. Many more details are most easily answered by the patent documentation itself or through an interview with the inventor or the patentee. While these answers are not sufficient to complete the valuation, the production of the necessary inputs to quantify the relevant cash flows and begin the valuation process is best informed by this approach.

Finally, any valuation of IP must take into account the extent to which the new owner is committed to defend it, both psychologically and financially.

Patented Technology Benchmarks and Remaining Useful Life

The data below only include instances where patents were specifically listed in the PPA and their remaining useful life was provided. If patents were not separately itemized in the PPA, they were not included in the statistics below. In one example, patents were lumped with trademarks and trade names and given a remaining useful life of 30 years; that PPA was excluded from the analysis, as such a combination is not recommended.

Patents (Patents, Patent Licenses, Patented Technology)

Useful Life		**Value as Percentage of Total Intangible Assets**	
# Observations:	46	# Observations:	121
Average:	8.3 years	Average:	19.1%
25th percentile:	5.0 years	25th percentile:	1.6%
Median:	7.0 years	Median:	7.1%
75th percentile:	10.0 years	75th percentile:	23.3%
Mode:	5.0 years		

Value as Percentage of Identifiable Intangible Assets		**Value as Percentage of Business Selling Price**	
# Observations:	121	# Observations:	121
Average:	35.2%	Average:	17.8%
25th percentile:	6.3%	25th percentile:	1.3%
Median:	18.6%	Median:	6.6%
75th percentile:	58.3%	75th percentile:	20.0%

B. COMPUTER SOFTWARE

Computer software and program formats acquired in a business combination that are protected legally, such as by patent or copyright, meet the contractual-legal criterion for identification as intangible assets. PPAs refer to this software in many ways: acquired software, purchased software, developed software, etc. Many times the software valued is included in a developed technology asset.

Eric Thornton, now at Cambridge Associates, gave a presentation at ASA International in 2002 that gave a good outline of factors analysts should consider in valuing software in business combinations.

Types of Software

- System software;
- Utilities: antivirus, backup;
- Business operation applications:
  - ERP; and
  - Workflow.

- Office automation:
  - Accounting: payroll, general ledger, accounts payable;
  - Workflow; and
  - WP, spreadsheet, presentation, etc.
- Manufacturing and manufacturing controls (bill of materials, inventory control):
  - ERP; and
  - Logistics support.
- Engineering:
  - Design and rendering.
- Training:
  - Tutorials;
  - e-learning; and
  - Foreign language.
- Educational/recreational, reference (encyclopedia, atlas), games.

Factors to consider are organized by valuation approach:

Approaches/Methods

Cost Approach

- Reproduction cost vs. replacement cost;
- Trended historical cost method; and
- Software engineering model method

  Software engineering models:
  "Software engineering models are used to estimate effort (e.g., in person-months) to develop software based on (1) metric data (e.g., lines of source code) and (2) other attributes of the software and the software development environment." (Robert Reilly et al., Willamette Management Associates, *Valuation of Intangible Assets for Fair Value Accounting Purposes*, 2009)

  - COCOMO, a constructive cost model developed by Barry W. Boehm, Software Engineering Economics, 1981;
  - COCOMO II—1997, recalibrated annually, Center for Software Engineering, University of Southern California;
  - SLIM, Software Lifecycle Management, a licensed software cost estimation tool developed by Quantitative Software Management Inc.; and
  - Checkpoint/KnowledgePLAN, a licensed software cost estimation tool developed by Software Productivity Research LLC.

Typical software engineering model inputs:

- Metrics
  - Lines of code;
  - Function points (IFPUG, Mk II);
  - Feature points (SPR);
  - Platform/environment;
  - Hardware, operating system; and
  - Language, tools, utilities.
- Development practices
  - *Product-related:*
    - Type of application;
    - Complexity, required reliability; and
    - Lifecycle (debugging, documentation).
  - *Personnel-related:*
    - Capability and experience; and
    - Fully loaded costs.

Income Approach

- Income or cost savings;
- Discounted cash flow method:
  - Need identifiable income stream;
  - Usually used for product software or databases that are sold or licensed;
  - Project income, expenses (excluding amortization/depreciation), and capital expenditures over remaining economic life (may differ from tax life);
  - Include capital charge when additional assets are used to produce the revenues. (See discussion of entrepreneurial incentive or opportunity cost below.); and
  - Discount to a present value.
- Relief from royalty method:
  - Similar to DCF but project cost savings to the owner, who would otherwise have to pay royalties on revenues earned from the asset; and
  - Empirical analysis of market-derived royalty rates for comparable assets.

Market Approach

(Typically in IP valuation engagements, there are availability and comparability issues with the market approach.)

- *Market transaction method*
  - Arm's-length market transaction data;
  - Typically expressed as dollars per line of code or dollars per function point;

  - Apply to subject software lines of code or function points to estimate value;
  - Adjust for material differences between comparable and subject software; and
  - Due to lack of data available, often used only as reasonableness check.

- *Market replacement cost method*
  - Contemplates replacement cost of the software in the open market;
  - Cost of comparable commercial off-the-shelf software packages;
  - Request hypothetical proposals to develop comparable software;
  - Consider the value of proprietary rights; and
  - Obsolescence.

  When an intangible asset is less useful than its ideal replacement, its value should be adjusted to reflect loss of economic value due to:

    - *Functional obsolescence:* impairment of its functional utility according to current market standards;
    - *Technological obsolescence:* inefficient or outdated programming language or hardware;
    - *Economic obsolescence:* market conditions, competitors; and
    - *Physical deterioration:* not generally applicable to data processing intangibles.

Remaining Useful Life Analysis

Importance:

- Income approach—Analysts need to estimate the projection period;
- Cost approach—Analysts need to estimate the amount of obsolescence, if any; and
- Market approach—Analysts need to adjust the comparable/guideline transactional data.

Factors affecting expected remaining useful life of data processing intangible assets:

- Legal determinants;
- Contractual determinants;
- Functional determinants;
- Technological determinants;
- Economic determinants; and
- Analytical determinants.

Typical Remaining Useful Life Analysis Method

The theory of survivor curves was developed at Iowa State University in the early 1900s. (Pamela Garland and Robert Reilly of Willamette explain this in the special report *Trade Secrets Remaining Useful Life Analysis.*) Survivor curves are used to predict the mortality or decay of a group of similar assets (e.g., intellectual properties) as the assets age. Survivor curve theory is similar to the mortality table theory used by actuaries to estimate the human life span.

- Estimate historical attrition rate;
- Develop survivor curves based on historical attrition rates;
- Match subject survivor curves to Iowa (or other) curves, using least squares method; and
- Resulting curve and average life are used to predict future mortality.

For data processing intangibles:

- Data are not often available for this type of analysis; and
- Could examine "retirement" of lines of code (rewritten or replaced), objects, modules, programs, or subsystems.

Special Considerations

- Ownership (determination of ownership is the first step in due diligence for valuing intangibles):
  - Source code for software packages is frequently sold/licensed to companies that modify the programs; and
  - Do not include lines of code not owned in software engineering models.
- Remove obsolete code from analysis and do not count multiple copies/versions of same program (adjust for "cloning").

Software Development Life Cycle

- Consider which phases of the life cycle have been completed and which are included in the model you are using. Incomplete but planned processes may be valued as IPR&D.

The cost approach is many times the best approach when the asset is readily replaceable and the costs of replacement are reasonably determined, such as with internally developed software.

Sample Approach to Valuing Developed Software

Mark Zyla developed a detailed ASC 805 workshop for analysts in 2011 for Business Valuation Resources. He presented the following typical process for looking at developed software:

> Our client makes an acquisition. We're asked to measure the fair value of the identified assets for the target company. Let's say the acquired company internally developed some billing software five years ago, and it's considered an identified asset under the accounting rules, so we're asked to measure what's the fair value of that billing software.
>
> Now there are a number of various methods under the cost technique that we can look at that fair value of that software. One way we can look at, if the records exist, is how much time and effort was spent in developing that software, and, now that it's three years old, make some adjustments for obsolescence and so on.

Another way we can look at it is: what if we had to develop billing software today? What steps would we undergo to develop that software? We talk to the programmer and say, "If we ask you to start from scratch, the billing software, what would you do?"

"Well, we need administrative time. We need to develop a plan. We would need to hire programmers. We would need special programming software, and so on. Here are the steps and here's the number of man hours that would take to develop the billing software."

In that particular instance, what we're actually doing is not capturing the cost to replace or the cost of what we actually did. We want billing software, but we don't care how they did it five years ago. As analysts, if we're using that particular method, we need to capture the cost to re-create what that software does, not necessarily the software itself.

If we do go through that process, we'll end up with state-of-the-art billing software ... which is not actually what we have. We make adjustments off of that. Again, when examining the cost approach, keep in mind it's not that we're re-creating the exact asset. We're re-creating what that asset does, its function, and that's an important distinction. Importantly, it's okay in measuring fair value, and it's something that is more appropriate than the actual asset itself in many circumstances.

When looking at the cost approach, there are some costs to consider that escape scrutiny in many such examinations. The first one is developer's profit: if we were to capture all the costs that went into that software for that intangible asset, would we sell it for those total costs?

The likely answer is no, because we would want to capture some sort of profit or some additional value to us for the effort of incurring those costs and developing the software. In other words, for the billing software example, we're using the cost approach to re-create some billing software and we capture all the costs. Would we sell it for the sum of the materials that went into it—programmer time, the purchase of new computers, additional labor we had to hire etc.—under the exit notion?

The answer is we would likely want some profit protection going through the exercise.

More and more frequently, although there's still divergence in practice, valuation specialists are including developer's profit as part of cost in the cost approach.

Similarly, another cost that typically valuation specialists don't think of under the cost approach is something called the entrepreneurial incentive, sometimes referred to as opportunity cost. When our client is spending time and effort developing an asset, it is tying up capital, diverting it from otherwise productive uses. Isn't that a cost that should be included in that intangible asset, the cost of capital? More and more frequently, you're seeing valuation specialists include opportunity costs as it relates to cost of the capital tied up while that asset is being developed; that cost is sometimes referred to as entrepreneurial incentive.

Computer Software Benchmarks and Remaining Useful Life

Software			
Useful Life		**Value as Percentage of Total Intangible Assets**	
# Observations:	54	# Observations:	151
Average:	5.6 years	Average:	18.4%
25th percentile:	3.0 years	25th percentile:	2.4%
Median:	5.0 years	Median:	9.1%
75th percentile:	7.4 years	75th percentile:	24.6%
Mode:	5.0 years		
Value as Percentage of Identifiable Intangible Assets		**Value as Percentage of Business Selling Price**	
# Observations:	152	# Observations:	151
Average:	37.7%	Average:	17.5%
25th percentile:	7.1%	25th percentile:	2.0%
Median:	25.3%	Median:	8.1%
75th percentile:	63.1%	75th percentile:	22.0%

Note:

- Software companies with software the dominant asset acquired tend to skew the benchmarks upward, so be sure to consider the industry slices chapter

C. UNPATENTED TECHNOLOGY

Unpatented technology acquired in a business combination is recorded as an identifiable intangible asset with an associated deferred tax liability due to its separability. The intangible asset is amortized over its estimated useful life. For purposes of this study, unless a filer indicated the valued technology was patented, and the valuation of a patent took form, it was considered unpatented.

Weston Anson of Consor believes value of technology must be based on market conditions and any valuation should adapt itself to today's economic realities. Any method of valuation should be responsive to the rapidly changing technological realities in many industries, particularly in high-technology areas such as biotechnology and medical technology. Therefore, a system of calculating value based on cost or current profitability figures is not necessarily responsive to today's conditions.

The valuation analyst should consider all forms of obsolescence in a cost approach analysis:

1. *Physical deterioration*—reduction in value due to physical wear and tear;
2. *Functional obsolescence*—reduction in value due to inability to perform the function (or yield the economic utility) for which the intangible asset was originally created;
3. *Technological obsolescence*—reduction in value due to improvements in technology;
4. *External obsolescence*—reduction in value due to the effects, events, or conditions external to the subject intangible asset;

5. *Locational obsolescence*—reduction in value related to location of real property rights; and
6. *Economic obsolescence*—reduction in value related to the ability of the asset owner to earn a fair return.

In an instructive case, *Nestle Holdings v. Commissioner* (T.C. Memo 1995-441, 1995 Tax Ct. Memo LEXIS 439), the IRS contended that technologies were essentially worthless because they could not be sold separately from the Carnation plants. It contended further that the technologies were known outside Carnation. Thus the only valuation approach should be a cost approach estimating the cost of engineering services that would have been required to duplicate the technologies.

To the separate salability contention, the court responded, "We do not require transferability of an asset in order to conclude that a particular asset has a determinable value.... The cost method is generally used when other methods of valuation such as comparable sales or income capitalization are not applicable due to the uniqueness and non-income-producing use of the property.... Here the technology in dispute was used for the production of various Carnation products and thus was income-producing property. The use to which the property is put is relevant to the question of value."

The taxpayer's expert valued the technology based on the present value of the net cash flow attributable to the products that related to the technology. The IRS challenged the application of the DCF approach on the basis that the taxpayer's appraisal relied on management's representations and that "failure to consider industry knowledge of the Carnation technology resulted in a substantially overstated valuation." The IRS also contended that the calculation did not properly separate trademark and technology valuations, thus creating the probability that one or the other or both were overrated.

The court summarized with two key points:

- Carnation technology was unique in some respects, but the valuation report in all probability exaggerated the uniqueness, relying solely on Carnation management for the relevant information; and
- The valuator made no attempt to separate income attributable to going concern from income attributable to technology. The products were successful due to many factors such as reputation and distribution systems. (This is a common refrain, as valuators will attest.)

Technology Benchmarks and Remaining Useful Life

Technology

Useful Life		**Value as Percentage of Total Intangible Assets**	
# Observations:	271	# Observations:	618
Average:	7.1 years	Average:	21.2%
25th percentile:	5.0 years	25th percentile:	7.9%
Median:	6.0 years	Median:	16.0%
75th percentile:	9.2 years	75th percentile:	29.4%
Mode:	5.0 years		

Value as Percentage of Identifiable Intangible Assets		**Value as Percentage of Business Selling Price**	
# Observations:	620	# Observations:	629
Average:	44.6%	Average:	20.1%
25th percentile:	24.0%	25th percentile:	6.8%
Median:	43.5%	Median:	13.8%
75th percentile:	63.5%	75th percentile:	26.6%

Notes:

- Technology categories have more labels than any other identifiable intangible asset in purchase price allocations as analysts try to somehow define the purpose of the technology. As one analyst put it, technology is "as you define it." As another stated, "it's a muddle." For the most part, technology should be defined by its state of development: in process technology, generally referred to as IPR&D, developed technology and future technology (which may be reflected in a company valuation but is not an asset). Here are the labels analysts are using for technology:
  - Core technology is basic technology that a company expects to be using for some time, generally giving it a longer useful life. The 2001 IPR&D Practice Aid published by AICPA defined it as "[t]hose technical processes, intellectual property, and the institutional understanding that exist within an organization with respect to products or processes that have been completed and that will aid in the development of future products, services, or processes that will be designed in a manner to incorporate similar technologies." Because Topic 805 generally accepts these criteria for separate recognition of the intangible asset in a business combination, ASA is recommending not distinguishing "core technology."
  - Developed technology is completed technology, either for sale or for internal use, as contrasted with in process technology, which is technology not yet proven, not revenue generating, in various stages of testing, etc.
  - Existing technology is developed technology.
  - Acquired or purchased technology is self-explanatory and may well already have a remaining useful life but is categorized as developed technology for purposes of this study.

D. DATABASES

Databases are collections of information, often stored in electronic form (such as on computer disks or files). An acquired database that includes original works of authorship is entitled to copyright protection and, if so protected, meets the contractual-legal criterion for recognition apart from goodwill. However, a database often includes information created as a consequence of an entity's normal operations, such as a customer list or specialized information such as a title plant, scientific data, and credit information. Databases that are for some reason not protected by copyright can be (and often are) exchanged in their entirety or in part. Alternatively, they can be (and often are) licensed or leased to others. Thus, even if the future economic benefit of a database does not arise from legal rights, it meets the separability criterion for recognition as an asset apart from goodwill.

Database Benchmarks and Remaining Useful Life

Databases

Useful Life		**Value as Percentage of Total Intangible Assets**	
# Observations:	22	# Observations:	39
Average:	10.1 years	Average:	18.2%
25th percentile:	5.9 years	25th percentile:	2.9%
Median:	10.0 years	Median:	9.1%
75th percentile:	11.0 years	75th percentile:	22.0%
Mode:	10.0 years		
Value as Percentage of Identifiable Intangible Assets		**Value as Percentage of Business Selling Price**	
# Observations:	40	# Observations:	39
Average:	36.5%	Average:	16.7%
25th percentile:	7.4%	25th percentile:	2.9%
Median:	36.8%	Median:	10.5%
75th percentile:	53.1%	75th percentile:	23.2%

Notes:

- Content and databases were examined together to develop this analysis; and
- Readers should also review the chapter on copyrights.

Chapter 3. Trade Secrets

A trade secret is information that provides a business with a unique, competitive advantage. U.S. courts have allowed trade secret protection to formulae, recipes, business plans, designs, processes, software, and other know-how. Unfortunately for valuators, much of the law governing trade secrets emanates from the states and different courts may reach different conclusions concerning whether a presumed trade secret is protected.

A good definitional guideline is to look at what federal agencies generally use to base their allowance for redacting mandatory submissions of data, from Restatement of Torts, Section 757:

> A trade secret may consist of any formula, pattern, device or compilation of information which is used in one's business, and which gives him an opportunity to obtain an advantage over competitors who do not know or use it.

Whereas a patent requires sharing of key information with the public, protecting trade secrets requires an effort to keep that information secret. By way of explanation, if you decide to patent a trade secret, once the application or patent is published, it will no longer be protected by trade secret laws. Accordingly, for a specific IP, you have to choose between patent protection and trade secret protection. Of course, you can protect trade secrets that relate to a patented IP, and you can strategically time the patent filing until later in the process, as many do, all the time protecting your trade secrets. Patent protection provides a stronger IP protection; patents can be enforced against someone who independently develops or reverse engineers an innovation. Perhaps more importantly, patents provide a defensive protection by being prior art so that someone else can't obtain patent rights to the invention. For these reasons, you will see IT management strategies that first protect inventions as trade secrets and later at a good strategic time file for patent protection.

Here are six factors to be considered in determining whether given information is a trade secret:

1. The extent to which the information is known outside the secret holder's business;
2. The extent to which the information is known by employees and others involved in the business;

3. The extent of measures taken by the secret holder to guard the secrecy of the information. (Important: If minimal efforts are taken to keep a secret, the data gathered in Points No. 1 and No. 2 can be rendered moot.);
4. The value of the information to the secret holder and to competitors;
5. The amount of effort or money expended by the secret holder in developing the information (its cost);
6. The ease or difficulty with which the information could be properly acquired or duplicated by others.

Valuators of trade secrets need to determine whether steps have been taken to keep them secret. It is a good idea to look for at least four related procedures:

1. All employees, independent contractors, and consultants should sign confidentiality agreements.
   a. This extends to exiting employees as well, as manifested in noncompete and nondisclosure agreements. (Noncompete agreements have their own set of valuation criteria and are treated separately in this research.)
2. Employee handbooks should contain confidentiality sections.
3. All of the information a company considers secret should be isolated so that only authorized individuals have access.
4. Communications to employees should stress:
   a. Any information or know-how developed while in the employ of the company belongs to the company;
   b. The company intends to enforce its rights with respect to its trade secrets; and
   c. The nature of the company's trade secrets, how they are being protected, and how important they are to the company (how the company would be damaged should the secrets be revealed).

Typically, trade secrets will generate incremental value in one of five ways:

1. *Revenue generation:* Trade secrets will provide some barrier to entry, enabling their owner to extract abnormal profits from selling a product or service in the market that uses a trade secret. For example, a company sells an effective liquid cleaner. A trade secret protects the formulation. The formulation allows the trade secret order to generate revenues in excess of other less effective cleaners in the market, despite the fact that costs to produce the cleaner are similar to competing products.
2. *Revenue preservation:* The trade secret will prevent negative information from becoming public, thereby preserving the continuance of revenues. Imagine what would result from the revelation to all of a company's customers that it was offering a sizable discount to Customer A.

3. *Cost savings:* The trade secret will provide some advantage to the owner, creating some type of ongoing cost savings that competitors may not have. Let's say BeefCo has developed a genetic program over several decades to generate a pure line of beef that has a greater feed conversion ratio than the broader market. BeefCo can grow its cattle to mature condemnation weight for substantially less feed costs. Suppose this creates an annual feed costs reduction that yields $5 million in free cash flow. Suppose further that BeefCo's discount rate is 25% and that this cost reduction is practically perpetual. This would indicate that the present value of BeefCo's trade secrets is $20 million as it relates to feed cost savings.

4. *Risk reduction:* The trade secret will provide some reduction in the risk that its owner would have to incur to generate cash flows. For example, suppose that a company intends to create a new medical device that detects blood glucose in a continuous monitoring system. The device will require FDA approval. A company that seeks to survive this testing, having never gone through it before, is at greater risk of failure than one that has been through the process already; the knowledge of preparing and performing the clinical trials is a trade secret for a company because it would reduce the risk for the company of getting the product to market successfully. Risk reduction creates value.

5. *Time acceleration:* Trade secrets can help create value in two forms because that value relates to time acceleration. Recall that a dollar today is worth more than it is in the future because of the time value of money. A trade secret that can accelerate the time to receiving cash flow can create value for the trade secret owner. For example, if a trade secret allows a company to get a product to the market one year sooner, the value relates to this time acceleration because it is receiving revenue sooner than it would otherwise pass.

Floor Values

For a competing company to overcome the barriers imposed by trade secrets, the company would have to invest both time and money, an investment establishing a floor on the value of the trade secrets (the value of the trade secret can be no less than a floor value, if there is value). The floor value consists of two primary components: the replacement cost to re-create a trade secret plus the opportunity cost for the investment in time and money, or:

Trade secret floor value = replacement cost + opportunity cost

Qualifying as an Intangible Asset for PPA Purposes

If the future economic benefit of an acquired trade secret is protected legally, such as by the Uniform Trade Secrets Act, the Economic Espionage Act of 1966, or a multitude of state laws and regulations, that asset meets the contractual-legal criterion for recognition as an asset apart from goodwill. (In an April 2012 case, the Federal Circuit Court of Appeals, 2nd Circuit, overturned a conviction under the EEA stating that, unless the trade secret was designed for interstate or foreign commerce, the statute did not apply. This calls into question how any trade secret could be protected by the Economic Espionage Act of 1966.) Otherwise, a trade secret would be recognized as an asset apart from goodwill only if the separability criterion was met, which is still likely to be the case.

The National Science Foundation (NSF) and the U.S. Census Bureau co-sponsored a 2008 survey of U.S. businesses as part of a revamped and expanded Business R&D and Innovation Survey (BRDIS). The BRDIS collects information from a nationally representative sample of about 40,000 companies, including companies in both manufacturing and nonmanufacturing industries.

Fourteen percent of surveyed businesses reported trade secrets as very important or somewhat important at 6% and 8%, respectively (see Exhibit 3).

Exhibit 3. 2008 BRDIS Survey

	All businesses			Businesses with R&D activity			Businesses without R&D activity		
IIPR, Industry, and NAICS code	Very	Somewhat	Not	Very	Somewhat	Not	Very	Somewhat	Not
Trade secrets									
All industries	6	8	85	45	22	33	5	0	87
Chemicals, 325	50	17	33	60	13	19	33	20	47
Computer and electronic products, 334	36	18	46	58	25	17	17	12	71
Internet services, web search portals, and data processing services, 518	21	30	50	28	50	22	17	21	62
Electrical equipment, appliances, and components, 335	25	23	52	51	27	22	10	21	69
Food, 311	22	20	58	56	20	25	16	20	64
Publishing, 511	26	15	58	64	17	19	10	15	75

It is surprising, then, that only 11 of the more than 6,000 PPAs analyzed for this guide valued trade secrets.

Trade Secrets Benchmarks and Remaining Useful Life

Trade Secrets or Know-How

Useful Life
Observations: 11

Average:	8.3 years
25th percentile:	4.0 years
Median:	5.0 years
75th percentile:	8.0 years
Mode:	5.0 years

Value as Percentage of Identifiable Intangible Assets
Observations: 32

Average:	33.4%
25th percentile:	9.4%
Median:	26.1%
75th percentile:	46.1%

Value as Percentage of Total Intangible Assets
Observations: 32

Average:	16.3%
25th percentile:	5.0%
Median:	11.8%
75th percentile:	22.2%

Value as Percentage of Business Selling Price
Observations: 32

Average:	13.1%
25th percentile:	3.3%
Median:	6.9%
75th percentile:	17.0%

Chapter 4. Marketing Intangibles

Trademarks (and Trade Names)

Trademarks provide a vendor with a means to identify and/or differentiate goods and services from others in the market. Trademarks apply to products. Service marks apply to services. A trade name is the name under which any business is continuing. A trade name must be attached to a business. A trademark is differentiable from a trade name in that it is used in association with salable goods or services. Trade names may be applied to or used in association with goods or services but only to indicate the marketing or trading entity. A trade name might also be a trademark; a trader may use more than a trademark, but a business is generally represented by a single, constant trade name. In 20% of purchase price allocations, trademarks and trade names are lumped together as an intangibles class.

Unlike patents and copyrights, trademarks protect only the symbol (or phrase, device, etc.) attached to the goods, not the goods themselves. The trademark's owner is entitled only to prevent that mark from being used to make purchasers believe they are buying the trader's goods when, in fact, they are buying a competitor's (likelihood of confusion).

In general, trademarks reduce buyer search costs (i.e., the costs a buyer incurs to find a product or service that meets the buyer's need). If a trademark has value, it will increase the free cash flow of the firm that the seller would not otherwise generate. If the trademark cannot increase free cash flow, then it may have no value to the firm. If the trademark prevents the generation of free cash flow, it may actually impair the firm's value.

Trademarks create value in any combination of the following three ways or variants thereof:

- *Lower sales and marketing costs:* Trademarks reduce buyer search costs because buyers might not have to spend as much time finding a product that they trust—buyers trust the brand or trademark associated with the product or service. This translates directly into value for a seller of a good or service because it might expend incrementally fewer dollars to close a deal, compared with competitors in the market. For example, in 2008, Starbucks had 16,680 locations (i.e., company-owned stores and licensed retailers) and generated $9.94 billion from those locations. That equates to average revenue per location of about $596,000. Starbucks spent $129 million in advertising, or about $7,733 per location, which is roughly 1.3% of total revenues. A typical food service industry spends 2% to 5% of total revenues on advertising. This means that Starbucks sells coffee that requires less marketing expenditures than what might be typical for local coffee retailers because it has established a strong brand experience for its customers. Thus, Starbucks has a competitive advantage of 0.7% to 3.7% because of its strong brand.

- *Greater revenues:* Trademarks have an uncanny ability to instill value in the eyes of the buyer. This value can translate directly into the ability of the seller to charge the buyer a premium for its good or service over competitors. Morton is able to charge a premium for its otherwise generic sodium chloride (i.e., salt) because it has built a brand in the eyes of the buyer. An attorney with a stellar reputation is able to charge a premium over other attorneys because of that stellar reputation. This can easily amount to hundreds of thousands of dollars in earnings for the attorney. Starbucks can charge much more for a cup of coffee compared to local retailers (e.g., convenience stores) in part because of its strong brand.

- *Greater market share or faster market adoption*: Trademarks can create market share for a seller or assist the seller in getting to the market faster. This translates directly into value for a seller of a good or service because it might generate an incrementally greater product sales volume, compared with competitors in the market. Again, consider Starbucks. It has greater market share in part because of its strong brand, which it calls the "Starbucks Experience." The Starbucks Experience builds product loyalty, which relates directly to Starbucks' trademarks.

The reason that young trademarks (i.e., new trademarks applied to products or services that have a relatively short history of use) do not command much value is because they do not yet create value for the seller. Young trademarks generally require significant investments in marketing to create associated goodwill, often greater than existing products that already have traction. Next, young trademarks have not yet had the time to create value in the eyes of the buyer; thus, whether the trademark creates value may be unclear (especially with introductory pricing on new products). Lastly, young trademarks will not command significant market share or adoption because they are new to the market and require time to build confidence and trust in the eyes of the buyer.

In a trademark valuation engagement, the analyst should consider all three of the trademark value sources to determine any possible value attributable to the trademark.

Trademark due diligence is somewhat less complicated than other intellectual property types because relatively fewer factors can derail trademarks administratively. Possible due diligence activity for trademarks includes the following tasks:

- Verify the history and creation of the trademark;
- Verify the trademark registration; and
- Verify the trademark status.

Continued Use

Patents, copyrights, and trade secrets do not have any explicit requirements for use of the intellectual property to preserve ongoing government protections. The company, at its pleasure, can establish vast portfolios of patents, copyrights, or trade secrets, perhaps never monetizing them, yet still preserve basic protections for the statutory or economic life of each IP type. This is not the case for trademarks, which require continued use by a company as a condition of registration under 15 U.S.C. §1051.

The continued use requirement has an obvious reason. Without the continued use requirement, people or companies would register trademarks for products or services that they never had any intention of marketing and hoard them, much like cybersquatters operate today with Internet domain names. Cybersquatters are people or companies that register literally thousands of Internet domain names that derive from the goodwill associated with trademarked goods or services and seek to resell those domain names to the trademark owners. Cybersquatters capitalize on the relatively low cost of registration (often only several dollars), purchasing them with the hopes of reselling them to other companies at large profits. Companies that refuse to pay the cybersquatters might face the prospect of their posting of derogatory information about the companies on the squatted websites.

Thus, for a trademark to maintain a value to its owner, the trademark owner must attest to continued use of the mark to receive continued protection. Moreover, this use must constitute more than mere token activity, such as selling 10 copies of a product using the trademark to a relative across state lines. Failure by the trademark owner to confirm continued use would allow a petitioner to request that the USPTO cancel the existing registration because the registrant is violating the continued use requirement.

Public Notice

Under 15 U.S.C. §1117(b), a trademark owner may collect treble profits or damages from infringers when the facts demonstrate that infringement was intentional. An important part of proving intentional infringement is to provide systematic notice of trademark registrations, with a "TM" mark, an "SM" mark, or the "®" mark.[3] Failure to provide notice opens the door to a claim of innocent infringement, a defense strategy by an accused trademark infringer that his or her infringement was accidental and the person did not realize he or she was infringing the protected work. As with a copyrighted work, an accused infringer can mount this strategy if the infringed work does not provide proper notice.

The value impact of failing to provide notice of a trademark registration can be large—a trademark owner might recover only one-third of potential damages because the court might not find that the trademark owner provided sufficient notice to the public regarding the trademark registration. Thus, providing notice can improve value by reducing the chances of impairing a possible judgment because of an innocent infringement defense.

Practically, the valuation analyst will query the trademark owner to verify that it is providing proper notice to the public of its registered mark. The valuation analyst should inspect samples of products and marketing materials that use the trademark to ensure conformance.

3 Richard Stim, *Patent, Copyright, and Trademark: An Intellectual Property Desk Reference*, 9th ed., Nolo, Berkeley, Calif., 2007, p. 410.

The valuation analyst must understand the durability of the trademark in relation to positive and negative news. Several factors are important in this consideration:

- *Does the trademark address a single product or a family of products?* A trademark that represents a single product carries a higher degree of volatility than a trademark that represents a family of products. This is because the trademark receives the diversification associated with a portfolio when applied to a family of products. If one product covered by a trademark disappoints the market and violates trust, such as the Ford Pinto, it may well kill that product in the market. However, the failure of the Ford Pinto may not bring down the entire Ford Motor Co. Trademarks that apply to a single product represent a single-source income stream that lacks diversification. Thus, a single-product trademark carries a greater risk than a trademark that applies to product families.

- *Can the trademarked product or service kill the buyer or create serious financial hardship?* A trademark that represents products or services that can kill the buyer (e.g., tainted Tylenol capsules) or create serious financial hardship (e.g., using Arthur Andersen as an auditor) might experience value impairment catastrophically. The trademark might never recover from such impairments, as was the case for Encaprin, Arthur Andersen, and the Chi-Chi's restaurant chain.

- *Is it common for competing products or services to maintain similar negative reputations?* Trademarks may not receive much value impairment in the event of unsatisfactory customer experiences if competing products or services maintain similar customer satisfaction levels. For example, a used car dealer with a buyer perception of being less than honest may still be able to survive because its competitors may also have a buyer perception of being less than honest. Thus, the lack of viable buyer alternatives may nullify any potential value impairment to the original trademark owner.

Practically, the valuation analyst may account for the probability of trademark value impairment in several ways. The trademark owner may incur additional sales and marketing expenditures to regain buyer trust (e.g., corrective advertising). This increases costs and reduces free cash flows associated with the trademark. The trademark owner may have to lower prices for the marked product or service to motivate buyers to a sale. This reduces revenues and free cash flows associated with the trademark. The execution risk for the trademark owner monetizing the trademark can increase as well. This puts upward pressure on the discount rate associated with the free cash flows derived from the trademark, which generates a corresponding value reduction.

Incontestability

Under 15 U.S.C. §1065, a registered trademark owner's mark is incontestable after five years from the registration date. This means that another trademark owner cannot dispute the trademark's registration, claiming interference for example on a similar good or service. Incontestability provides a trademark owner with a more valuable trademark because the probability of a third party breaking the trademark exists. Thus, as long as the trademark owner fulfills the basic administrative functions associated with trademark ownership (e.g., continued usage, payment of maintenance fees, etc.), it can maintain perpetual ownership of the associated trademark rights. Moreover, no third party could contest the trademark rights.

Thus, an important part of trademark exploitation is the consistent use of the trademark in the market to reinforce consumer trust. This might include everything from white spacing requirements used in association with the mark to colors used to printing specifications. The inconsistent use of the mark in the market can create confusion for buyers, thereby depressing trademark value.

Trademark Strength

Several factors drive the strength of trademarks. Recall that the stronger the trademark, the more value it can command in the market. Trademark strength can manifest in several forms (i.e., a marked product commands a greater price in the market). Valuation analysts should be interested in trademark strength from the perspective of how easily a third party could challenge and defeat the mark's protections and/or derive economic benefits from the registered mark, thereby usurping economic opportunity from the trademark's owner.

In addition, the valuation analyst should consider several factors relating to the strength of the trademark, including the type of trademark and the trademark age.

Trademark type has a specific meaning in a legal context that lends directly to trademark strength. Arising from the *Abercrombie & Fitch Co. v. HuntingWorld, Inc.* decision, these trademark types include generic marks, descriptive marks, suggestive marks, and arbitrary and fanciful marks, in what the industry knows as the spectrum of distinctiveness.[4] The following is an overview of each:

- *Generic marks:* Generic trademarks are just that: generic. They refer to trademarks to which one attempts to assign secondary meaning, though such attempts will always fail because the marks describe an entire group of products. Consumers would not be able to distinguish one product from another. Famous generic marks include aspirin and escalator. The valuation analyst must always conclude that generic trademarks have no value because there is nothing protectable to consider.

- *Descriptive marks:* Descriptive marks can be valuable when they take on a secondary meaning. Ordinarily, trademark applicants cannot receive trademark registrations on descriptive items (e.g., the "Yellow" phone book). The only way that registrants can receive trademark protection is if the trademark takes on a secondary meaning (i.e., some public meaning beyond the obvious meaning of terms or images that comprise the trademark). Restaurants such as McDonald's thrive on secondary meaning for fast-food restaurants that promise a user experience, thereby preventing another person with the last name of McDonald from opening a similar type of restaurant. Such marks can become quite valuable; however, they can take decades to develop and require significant sales and marketing investment. For nascent marks, the valuation analyst should ensure that an appropriate budget of resources matches the market intent for the trademark as used in the market.

4 *Abercrombie & Fitch, Co. v. HuntingWorld, Inc.*, 537 F.2d 4, 9 (2nd Cir. 1976).

- *Suggestive marks:* Suggestive marks bring to mind a quality or characteristic of the good or service that it represents. The idea is to tie the good or service mark to some image in the consumer's mind. For example, Florida's Natural branded orange juice suggests a wholesome goodness, made from natural ingredients. Such marks can become quite valuable, and they might get that value more easily, as the chances of the USPTO classifying the registration as descriptive are lower. However, they can also take decades to develop.
- *Arbitrary marks:* Arbitrary marks are generally very strong trademarks. These trademarks tend to describe goods or services that otherwise have no relation. For example, Amazon describes an Internet retailer as well as a jungle in South America. Such marks can become quite valuable over time; however, they can also attract unwanted attention and lawsuits. For example, Apple Corps Ltd., founded by the Beatles, sued Apple Computer several times and extracted significant settlements from Apple Computer because of its trademark drift into the music space, which Apple Corps Ltd. owned.
- *Fanciful marks:* Fanciful marks are generally the strongest trademarks one can own. These trademarks tend to describe goods or services and likely have no other precedent in the market. Pharmaceutical companies are famous for developing fanciful marks for various goods and services that they sell. Lipitor, Clarinex, Sarafem, Allegra, and literally hundreds of other products did not generally have precedents in the market. This is advantageous in several ways. First, the trademark registrant will likely receive no opposition from other parties because the risk of collision is low. Second, by having distinct names, the trademark registrant reduces the potential for medical errors. Third, all traditional trademark building tools are available, including sometimes tricky items such as domain names (recall the problems with nissan.com). Fourth, having fanciful trademarks reduces the probability of a lawsuit from an unrelated brand (e.g., Nissan Motor Co. and Nissan Computer Corp.). Lastly, fanciful marks can influence significant buyer demand, despite the availability of generics (e.g., Tylenol versus generic counterparts) and can create remarkable long-term value. The largest risk for fanciful marks is the risk of genericide, which happens when the public moves from using a trademark in an adjective form to using it in a verb or noun form. For example, many people "google" an item they want to search on the Internet, as opposed to using the Google search engine to retrieve the answer. Such widespread adoption and misuse can destroy the associated value with a trademark. Several well-known nouns today, such as aspirin and escalator, were trademarks to their original inventors but have since crossed over into common usage. Today, these words are generic and maintain no trademark power.

Trademark age has a positive relationship with trademark strength as well. The older the trademark, the more likely it will be stronger, as historically trademark renewal rates averaged only about 27% between 1934 and 1999.[5] Additionally, older trademarks speak directly to the useful life of the trademark, since the trademark owners must maintain continual use of the trademarks to maintain protection.

5 William M. Landes and Richard A. Posner, *The Economic Structure of Intellectual Property Law*, The Belknap Press of Harvard University Press, Cambridge, Mass., 2003, p. 250.

Dilution

Recall that a trademark owner registers the trademark for a certain class of goods or services. Generally, a trademark owner cannot prevent others from using a similar mark for unrelated goods or services. However, if the trademark proves to be famous, then a trademark owner might be able to prevent a third party from using the similar mark because it might aid dilution of the primary trademark. Under 15 U.S.C. §1125, the IP valuation analyst can find the definition of famousness:

> (A) For purposes of paragraph (1), a mark is famous if it is widely recognized by the general consuming public of the United States as a designation of source of the goods or services of the mark's owner. In determining whether a mark possesses the requisite degree of recognition, the court may consider all relevant factors, including the following:
>
> > (i) The duration, extent, and geographic reach of advertising and publicity of the mark, whether advertised or publicized by the owner or third parties.
> >
> > (ii) The amount, volume, and geographic extent of sales of goods or services offered under the mark.
> >
> > (iii) The extent of actual recognition of the mark.

Counterfeit Risk

Counterfeits present value impairment risk for a trademark owner. Counterfeits are unauthorized reproductions, also known as knock-offs, of products or services represented by a strong trademark.

Market Dynamism

The dynamics of the particular market for a trademark can play an important role in trademark value. These dynamics can include the market size, the cost of information, and the cost of recognition.[6] First, the market size has a large impact on trademark value. The larger the applicable market, the larger the number of potential buyers for the products, thus, the greater the brand value potential. For example, suppose that a trademark owner earns $1 in contribution margin attributable to the trademark for a product. If the trademark owner sells one million units in a year, then the trademark owner will generate $1 million in that year, attributable to the trademark. If the trademark owner sells 100 million units in a year, then the trademark owner will generate $100 million in that year attributable to the trademark. The market size dictates the economic opportunity. General Electric (GE) likely has a strong brand in light bulbs that represents a significant number of units shipped annually. The GE brand for light bulbs is valuable.

The second major market driver for a trademark relates to the cost of information. The higher the cost of information relating to a product, the more difficult it is for a buyer to evaluate the product. Thus, the buyer is willing to trust the brand of the seller more. This is especially important in large fragmented markets with many vendors.

A third major market driver for trademark value relates to the cost of recognition. The more recognizable the trademark, the more valuable it becomes.

6 Id. at 64-65.

Legal Life

A trademark's legal life is indefinite, and special circumstances would have to exist for the remaining useful life of a trademark to be anything but that. In some cases, a PPA reveals an amortization schedule of a finite number of years. Immediate questions result. Are there plans to cease maintenance of the trademarks/trade names? Why? Did that plan factor into the valuation? Is there any other reason the trademarks have been assigned finite lives? For example, did the purchase and sale agreement for the business combination stipulate a time limitation on the trademark? If yes, what other limitations on the intangible assets purchased are reflected in the agreement?

Relief From Royalty

Relief from royalty approach to valuation assumes that, by owning a trademark, a company is relieved of the necessity of having to license it from someone else. A company wanting to obtain the right to this trademark would have to enter into a license agreement with the current owner. Such arrangements generally include a variable royalty rate for calculating remuneration, often a percentage of gross or net sales. The percentage will vary depending on the value factors mentioned in this chapter.

Trademarks (Trade Names) Benchmarks and Remaining Useful Life

Trademarks (Alone)

Useful Life	
# Observations:	75
# Indefinite:	22
# Amortized:	53
Average:	9.3 years
25th percentile:	4.0 years
Median:	7.0 years
75th percentile:	13.0 years
Mode:	4.0 years

Value as Percentage of Identifiable Intangible Assets	
# Observations:	176
Average:	25.0%
25th percentile:	4.3%
Median:	10.9%
75th percentile:	32.3%

Value as Percentage of Total Intangible Assets	
# Observations:	174
Average:	15.1%
25th percentile:	1.7%
Median:	4.6%
75th percentile:	14.9%

Value as Percentage of Business Selling Price	
# Observations:	171
Average:	13.6%
25th percentile:	1.4%
Median:	3.7%
75th percentile:	14.4%

Trade Names (Alone)

Useful Life

# Observations:	189
# Indefinite:	53
# Amortized:	136
Average:	7.9 years
25th percentile:	3.0 years
Median:	5.0 years
75th percentile:	10.0 years
Mode:	5.0 years

Value as Percentage of Identifiable Intangible Assets

# Observations:	472
Average:	23.1%
25th percentile:	4.3%
Median:	14.1%
75th percentile:	36.2%

Value as Percentage of Total Intangible Assets

# Observations:	472
Average:	11.4%
25th percentile:	1.6%
Median:	6.0%
75th percentile:	16.7%

Value as Percentage of Business Selling Price

# Observations:	475
Average:	8.4%
25th percentile:	1.4%
Median:	4.4%
75th percentile:	11.9%

Note:

- When a trademark or trade name was identified as an intangible asset and treated alone, there were only two purchase price allocations, which included both as an identifiable intangible asset. In one case, a value was assigned to the "corporate trade name" and a separate, distinct value assigned to "product trademarks." In the other case, one value was assigned to a "trade name" and another to the "trademark." Over 25% of the PPAs that identified trademarks or trade names lumped them into a single category. As the benchmarks above indicate, if there are both trademarks and trade names to account for, they require separate analyses.

Trademarks and Trade Names (A Combined Intangible)			
Useful Life		**Value as Percentage of Total Intangible Assets**	
# Observations:	90	# Observations:	218
# Indefinite:	20		
# Amortized:	70		
		Average:	10.6%
		25th percentile:	1.7%
Average:	8.9 years	Median:	5.2%
25th percentile:	5.0 years	75th percentile:	12.3%
Median:	8.5 years		
75th percentile:	10.0 years	**Value as Percentage of Business Selling Price**	
Mode:	10.0 years	# Observations:	220
Value as Percentage of Identifiable Intangible Assets			
# Observations:	219	Average:	8.7%
		25th percentile:	1.4%
		Median:	4.2%
Average:	22.9%	75th percentile:	10.1%
25th percentile:	1.6%		
Median:	6.0%		
75th percentile:	16.7%		

Notes:

- "Marketing intangibles" was treated as a combination of trademarks and trade names.
- One PPA inexplicably combined patents with trademarks and trade secrets, applying a 30-year remaining useful life. The data were excluded from this analysis.
- Several PPAs combined the valuation of a noncompete agreement with that of a trademark or trade name. Those data were excluded from this analysis.

ARTISTIC INTANGIBLES

Artistic-related intangible assets meet the criteria for recognition apart from goodwill if the assets arise from contractual rights or legal rights such as those provided by copyright. In the United States, for example, the government grants copyrights for the life of the creator plus 70 years (for works after Jan. 1, 1978). Copyrights can be transferred either in whole through assignments or in part through licensing agreements. In determining the fair value of an intangible asset protected by copyright, consideration shall be given to the existence of any assignments or licenses of the acquired copyrights. The FASB Statement does not preclude an acquiring entity from recognizing a copyright intangible asset and any related assignments or license agreements as a single intangible asset for financial reporting purposes if their useful lives are similar.

Copyright

Copyright is a form of protection provided by the laws of the United States (title 17, *U.S. Code*) to the authors of "original works of authorship," including literary, dramatic, musical, artistic, and certain other intellectual works. This protection is available to both published and unpublished works. Section 106 of the 1976 Copyright Act generally gives the owner of copyright the exclusive right to do and to authorize others to do the following:

- To reproduce the work in copies or phonorecords;
- To prepare derivative works based upon the work;
- To distribute copies or phonorecords of the work to the public by sale or other transfer of ownership, or by rental, lease, or lending;
- To perform the work publicly, in the case of literary, musical, dramatic, and choreographic works, pantomimes, and motion pictures and other audiovisual works;
- To display the work publicly, in the case of literary, musical, dramatic, and choreographic works, pantomimes, and pictorial, graphic, or sculptural works, including the individual images of a motion picture or other audiovisual work; and
- In the case of sound recordings, to perform the work publicly by means of a digital audio transmission.

Copyright protection subsists from the time the work is created in fixed form. The copyright in the work of authorship immediately becomes the property of the author who created the work. Only the author or those deriving their rights through the author can rightfully claim copyright. In the case of works made for hire, the employer and not the employee is considered to be the author. Section 101 of the copyright law defines a "work made for hire" as:

1. A work prepared by an employee within the scope of his or her employment; or
2. A work specially ordered or commissioned for use as:
    - A contribution to a collective work;
    - A part of a motion picture or other audiovisual work;
    - A translation;
    - A supplementary work;
    - A compilation;
    - An instructional text;
    - A test;
    - Answer material for a test; or
    - An atlas.
3. If the parties expressly agree in a written instrument signed by them that the work shall be considered a work made for hire.

The authors of a joint work are co-owners of the copyright in the work, unless there is an agreement to the contrary.

Copyright in each separate contribution to a periodical or other collective work is distinct from copyright in the collective work as a whole and vests initially with the author of the contribution.

Mere ownership of a book, manuscript, painting, or any other copy or phonorecord does not give the possessor the copyright. The law provides that transfer of ownership of any material object that embodies a protected work does not of itself convey any rights in the copyright.

Minors may claim copyright, but state laws may regulate the business dealings involving copyrights owned by minors.

Legal Lives

On or after Jan. 1, 1978 ...

A work that was created (fixed in tangible form for the first time) on or after Jan. 1, 1978, is automatically protected from the moment of its creation and is ordinarily given a term enduring for the author's life plus an additional 70 years after the author's death. In the case of "a joint work prepared by two or more authors who did not work for hire," the term lasts for 70 years after the last surviving author's death. For works made for hire, and for anonymous and pseudonymous works (unless the author's identity is revealed in Copyright Office records), the duration of copyright will be 95 years from publication or 120 years from creation, whichever is shorter.

Before Jan. 1, 1978 ...

Works originated but not published or registered by Jan. 1, 1978, have been automatically brought under the Copyright Act and are now given federal copyright protection. The duration of copyright in these works is generally computed in the same way as for works created on or after Jan. 1, 1978: the life-plus-70 or 95-/120-year terms apply to them as well. The law provides that in no case would the term of copyright for works in this category expire before Dec. 31, 2002, and for works published on or before Dec. 31, 2002, the term of copyright will not expire before Dec. 31, 2047.

Works originally created and published or registered before Jan. 1, 1978, need special attention: Copyright was secured either on the date a work was published with a copyright notice or on the date of registration if the work was registered in unpublished form. In either case, the copyright endured for a first term of 28 years from the date it was secured. During the last (28th) year of the first term, the copyright was eligible for renewal. The Copyright Act of 1976 extended the renewal term from 28 to 47 years for copyrights that were subsisting on Jan. 1, 1978, or for pre-1978 copyrights restored under the Uruguay Round Agreements Act (URAA), making these works eligible for a total term of protection of 75 years. Public Law 105-298, enacted on Oct. 27, 1998, further extended the renewal term of copyrights still subsisting on that date by an additional 20 years, providing for a renewal term of 67 years and a total term of protection of 95 years. Public Law 102-307, enacted on June 26, 1992, amended the 1976 Copyright Act to provide for automatic renewal of the term of copyrights secured between Jan. 1, 1964, and Dec. 31, 1977. Although the renewal term is automatically provided, the Copyright Office does not issue a renewal certificate for these works unless a renewal application and fee are received and registered in the Copyright Office.

Public Law 102-307 makes renewal registration optional. Thus, filing for renewal registration is no longer required to extend the original 28-year copyright term to the full 95 years. However, some benefits accrue to renewal registrations that were made during the 28th year.

Transfer of Copyright

Any or all of the copyright owner's exclusive rights or any subdivision of those rights may be transferred, but the transfer of exclusive rights is not valid unless that transfer is in writing and signed by the owner of the rights conveyed or such owner's duly authorized agent. Transfer of a right on a nonexclusive basis does not require a written agreement.

A copyright may also be conveyed by operation of law and may be bequeathed by will or pass as personal property by the applicable laws of intestate succession.

Copyright is a personal property right, and it is subject to the various state laws and regulations that govern the ownership, inheritance, or transfer of personal property as well as terms of contracts or conduct of business. For information about relevant state laws, consult an attorney.

Transfers of copyright are normally made by contract. The Copyright Office does not have any forms for such transfers.

The law does provide for the recordation in the Copyright Office of transfers of copyright ownership. Although recordation is not required to make a valid transfer between the parties, it does provide certain legal advantages and may be required to validate the transfer as against third parties. For information on recordation of transfers and other documents related to copyright, see Circular 12, Recordation of Transfers and Other Documents.

Termination of Transfers

Under the previous law, the copyright in a work reverted to the author, if living, or, if the author was not living, to other specified beneficiaries, provided a renewal claim was registered in the 28th year of the original term. The present law drops the renewal feature except for works already in the first term of statutory protection when the present law took effect.

Instead, the present law permits termination of a grant of rights after 35 years under certain conditions by serving written notice on the transferee within specified time limits. For works already under statutory copyright protection before 1978, the present law provides a similar right of termination covering the newly added years that extended the former maximum term of the copyright from 56 to 95 years.

For further information, see circulars 15a and 15t.

Mike Pellegrino, writing in *BVR's Guide to Intellectual Property Valuation, Second Edition*, describes factors to consider in valuing copyrights.

A valuation analyst focuses copyright due diligence on several distinct areas. They include the following:

- Verifying the nature of the copyrighted material (i.e., does a copyright protect it?);
- Verifying the nature of the rights to value;
- Consideration of administrative issues that can impair copyright value;
- Special considerations for software; and
- Special considerations for semiconductor designs or masks.

The following sections explore these concepts further.

Nature of Copyrighted Material

In general, copyright protection under 17 U.S.C. §102(a) includes the following works of authorship:

- Architectural works;
- Dramatic works, including any accompanying music;
- Literary works;
- Motion pictures and other audiovisual works;
- Musical works, including any accompanying words;
- Pantomimes and choreographic works;
- Pictorial, graphic, and sculptural works; and
- Sound recordings.

Copyright law requires that a creator of a copyrightable work satisfy several requirements:

1. The work must be original.
2. The creator must fix the work in some tangible medium of expression. That is, the creator must put it onto some physical object. If the work is a book, the tangible medium of expression is the book's pages. If the work is a song, the tangible medium of expression may include sheet music or a CD-ROM containing an MP3 of the recording. If the work is a sculpture, the obvious tangible medium may be marble or bronze.
3. The work must have some creativity and not represent the mere regurgitation of some other work. For example, one author notes that a telephone white page directory is not likely creative because it involves some nondiscretionary alphabetic listing of telephone numbers. However, a custom layout of a Yellow Pages page with customer ads may exhibit originality and creativity, making it more likely to have copyright protection, though a valuation analyst should rely on qualified legal counsel to make such a determination.

For music, the nature of the copyrighted material can take several forms. A musician who composes a song and affixes it in a tangible medium has protected the sheet music, lyrics, song structure, and so on. However, the sound of the song is another distinct right that also receives copyright protection. The song's sound covers the musical arrangement as well as the way the song sounds. The sound can vary based on a variety of factors, including instruments selected, time signature used, venue, reverb, effects, and many others. The combinations of sounds one could use to represent the same song are literally infinite.

A client may misunderstand the applicability of copyright law, which can affect the scope of a valuation assignment. Under 17 U.S.C. §102(b), copyright law specifically excludes ideas, procedures, processes, systems, methods of operation, concepts, principles, or discoveries. Copyright law does protect the expression of such an item, however, but not the item itself, which patents and trade secrets usually protect. Thus, a valuation analyst cannot value a process or idea under copyright law since no such protection exists. Clients who hire valuation analysts may not always know the distinction, so it is important for the valuation analyst to clarify any such discrepancies because they may affect the client's expectation of a final deliverable work product.

There are varying degrees of copyright strength, like patents, which the public might consider strong (i.e., broad) or weak (i.e., very narrow). A strong copyright typically means that much original expression is in the work, such as a sculpture, painting, or new song. A thin copyright typically refers to a work that consists of little original expression, such as a book to teach general accounting processes, a history textbook, or a telephone book. In each of the latter examples, which one might consider factual works (more on factual works shortly), it will be easier to reproduce the essence of the work without direct infringement. Moreover, given their nature, thin copyrights might be the scope of greater fair use than with other works (more on fair use shortly). In short, thin copyrights are generally worth less than stronger copyrights, much like weaker patents are worth less than stronger patents. It is important for the valuation analyst to gauge the strength of the copyright (potentially with the help of outside legal counsel) to associate an appropriate risk and discount rate for the assignment.

Verifying the Nature of Rights to Value

Copyrights represent a set bundle of rights. Each right may have its own value proposition. The valuation analyst must determine which set of rights is the focus of the assignment. The rights may take several forms, including the following:

- The right to sell the work;
- The right to display the work;
- The right to make copies of the work; and
- The right to make derivative works of the original.

The method that the valuation analyst uses and the magnitude of the value proposition will generally vary based on the nature of the right under consideration. For example, consider the case of an author who owns a copyright on a manuscript. The author creates a manuscript and licenses the right to make copies of the manuscript, display it, and sell it in the open market to a book publisher in exchange for a defined financial arrangement including a running royalty based on book sales. The manuscript generates revenue and net income.

The doctrine of fair use centers on a tenet that limited copying of the expressive elements of a work is not infringement even though the copyright holder did not grant permission to perform the copying. Governed by 17 U.S.C. §107, copyrighted works that may have a higher degree of potential value impairment from fair use may include:

- Photographs;
- Dramatic plays;
- Artistic paintings;
- Cinematic movies;
- Musical recordings;
- News subscriptions; and
- Scholarly publications.

Each of these copyrighted work types make them candidates for fair use because each is generally the subject of criticism, comment, news reporting, teaching, scholarship, or research, which are permissible uses under copyright law.

Special Considerations for Computer Software

Computer software is unique among IP types in that it may simultaneously receive protection under patent and copyright law. (It's still quite controversial, but parts of computer software can be the subject of patents if the software integrates into a machine, is manufactured to perform a process, or if it manipulates data to achieve a practical application.) Copyright law also covers expression of software (i.e., the actual source code in raw or compiled form) from the moment the author fixes the work in tangible form, such as saving it to a computer's disk drive or printing it in hard copy form. Ordinarily, this should not create difficulty for the valuation analyst because the scope of the valuation assignment will delineate whether the property of interest in the valuation is the copyright or the patent. Practically, the expression of a patented idea in software may be incidental to the overall value of the software program, as one of ordinary skill in the art could likely reproduce the software just by reading the patent without ever having access to the original source code covered under copyright law. Moreover, one of ordinary skill in the art could reproduce the function the software intends to serve.

Software consists of both state (i.e., data) and behavior (i.e., functions that use data). Software programmers reflect the state using data structures to represent both simple and complex concepts. For example, the computer has a means to represent an abstract object such as a car with data. The data would signify the number of wheels the car has, its color, steering wheel position, heading, speed, and many other factors. The behavior of the car would represent things the car can actually do, such as steer left, steer right, accelerate, slow down, crash, etc. The data are of little value in software without functions to use that data. Importantly, the copyright protects the expression of how to implement a behavior and the state. It does not protect the utility behind it. Thus, in the car example, a software designer receives copyright protection for the expression of the car in software form, primarily through source code. However, the copyright does not protect the actual algorithm or means to steer left, steer right, accelerate, or perform any of the associated behaviors of the car.

As software programmers can represent state and behavior in literally an infinite number of ways, it makes it relatively easy for another company to originate something that provides the same utility without fear of an infringement action. This reduces the potential value that may accrue to the software, since one may be able to reproduce the expression of the state and behavior for a cost lower than what the original author may want to charge in the open market. The risk associated with future cash flows attributable to the software may also increase as well because it may be more difficult for a company to extract value from the software due to increased competition. The potential value impairment just described is not necessarily as important for some valuation assignments, particularly if the costs to reproduce the copyrighted software would include significant sums or take a company out of a competitive market for a protracted time.

Disclosure

Software developers who register their source code with the U.S. Copyright Office may be reticent to provide the original source code. The key reason for not doing so is to prevent the publication of key company trade secrets expressed in the source code that the copyright owner does not wish to introduce into the public view. Of course, the key reason to avoid full disclosure of the source code is that it would be easy for a competitor to review the registration with the U.S. Copyright Office and learn how a competitor implemented a key value-creating feature. This creates two problems for the copyright owner. First, it would be difficult to detect the copyright infringement for such activity. Second, the complete disclosure may erase any value-creating opportunity for the original software developer. For example, suppose that Microsoft developed a means to generate very large Excel workbooks that require minimal computer resources to process. Under such a situation, Microsoft may desire copyright protection for its source code, yet disclosing all of its source code would provide key competitors such as Corel's Quattro Pro X4 product with intimate knowledge of how Microsoft created its high-performing spreadsheet. If Corel were to have access to Microsoft's source code, Microsoft would potentially lose the ability to generate higher revenues typically associated with proprietary products. Fortunately for software developers, the U.S. Copyright Office does allow software developers to submit redacted source code (i.e., the author blanks out every other line in the source code, requiring a potential infringer to "fill in the blanks" for the redacted areas of the source code).

Special Considerations for Semiconductor Designs or Masks

Semiconductors are materials that form the basis for integrated circuits, which may collectively include memory chips, microprocessors, and other similar miniaturized electronic circuits. These integrated circuits contain miniature designs of electrical circuits that form a pattern etched into silicon by sophisticated equipment to form the basis of a product. To create a microprocessor, one must first design the circuits that comprise the microprocessor. The manufacturer will then create a mask that represents the design that the manufacturer then uses to etch the circuit design into the silicon, which becomes an integral part of the final product. For the novice, a semiconductor mask is akin to a film negative. It is a two- or three-dimensional arrangement of transistors, resistors, and other electrical components that form the basis for an integrated circuit design. It provides the pattern that manufacturing equipment uses to replicate the microprocessor design for production volumes. Since the electrical circuit designs represent a work of authorship, they receive protection under copyright law, specifically under 17 U.S.C. §§901-914. Codified in the Semiconductor Chip Protection Act of 1984 (semiconductor designs and masks did not receive copyright protection before this time), Congress provides protection with certain caveats.

In our observations, copyrights appear to be either an overlooked identifiable intangible asset or simply unidentifiable.

Our data show four allocations with a value for copyrights. However, there was only one observable instance that listed a useful life. For this reason, we show the useful life of that one observation, followed by the value of the all four observations.

Copyrights Benchmarks and Remaining Useful Lives

Copyrights			
Useful Life		**Value as Percentage of Total Intangible Assets**	
# Observations:	1	Observations #1:	33.3%
Useful life:	5.0 years	Observations #2:	71.7%
		Observations #3:	16.5%
Value as Percentage of Identifiable Intangible Assets		Observations #4:	3.4%
Observations #1:	100.0%	**Value as Percentage of Business Selling Price**	
Observations #2:	84.3%	Observations #1:	1.9%
Observations #3:	42.4%	Observations #2:	58.3%
Observations #4:	10.9%	Observations #3:	16.9%
		Observations #4:	3.5%

Note:

- Databases and software are essentially copyright assets, and those chapters should be reviewed for a more complete look at copyright assets.

Domain Name

An Internet domain name is a unique alphanumeric name that is used to identify a particular Internet address. Registration of a domain name associates the name with a website on the Internet and with a brand for the period the registration is in effect. Those registrations are renewable. Registered domain names meet the contractual-legal criterion.

Valuation of domain names depends upon how entwined the business brand is with the domain and how dependent upon e-commerce is the business. In our study, only nine of the PPAs identified domain name as an intangible.

Domain Names Benchmarks and Remaining Useful Lives

Domain Names			
Useful Life		**Value as Percentage of Total Intangible Assets**	
# Observations:	9	# Observations:	35
# Indefinite:	6		
# Amortized:	3		
		Average:	18.3%
		25th percentile:	0.8%
Observations #1:	19.0 years	Median:	4.3%
Observations #2:	10.0 years	75th percentile:	27.3%
Observations #3:	3.0 years		
Value as Percentage of Identifiable Intangible Assets		**Value as Percentage of Business Selling Price**	
# Observations:	35	# Observations:	35
		Average:	15.1%
Average:	39.6%	25th percentile:	0.9%
25th percentile:	2.0%	Median:	4.1%
Median:	21.7%	75th percentile:	26.6%
75th percentile:	82.6%		

Notes:

- Remaining useful life: indefinite term
- Domains as a percentage of total intangibles:

  The ratios were so disparate that three observations are presented independently, with categorization that may rationally apply.

  1. Internet-dependent: 79.25%
  2. Small part of the branding effort: 2.72%
  3. A minor part of the organization's PR effort only: 0.01%

Chapter 5. Customer-Related Intangibles

A customer list consists of information about customers such as names and contact information. A customer list also may be in the form of a database that includes other information about the customers such as their order history and demographic information. A customer list does not generally arise from contractual or other legal rights. However, customer lists are valuable and are frequently leased or exchanged. Therefore, an acquired customer list would meet the separability criterion for recognition apart from goodwill. An acquired customer list would *not* meet that criterion, however, if the terms of confidentiality or other agreements prohibit an entity from selling, leasing, or otherwise exchanging information about its customers.

Customer Lists Benchmarks and Remaining Useful Lives

Customer Lists

Useful Life	
# Observations:	30
Average:	10.6 years
25th percentile:	5.0 years
Median:	10.0 years
75th percentile:	17.0 years
Mode:	17.0 years

Value as Percentage of Total Intangible Assets	
# Observations:	176
Average:	30.9%
25th percentile:	8.0%
Median:	20.0%
75th percentile:	46.3%

Value as Percentage of Identifiable Intangible Assets	
# Observations:	176
Average:	56.7%
25th percentile:	26.0%
Median:	51.2%
75th percentile:	94.8%

Value as Percentage of Business Selling Price	
# Observations:	175
Average:	25.5%
25th percentile:	5.2%
Median:	13.9%
75th percentile:	36.3%

Customer Contracts

In its Statement on Business Combinations, the FASB made a distinction between customer relationships as established by contracts and self-standing customer relationships. If an entity establishes relationships with its customers through contracts, those customer relationships would arise from contractual rights. Therefore, customer contracts and the related customer relationships are intangible assets that meet the contractual-legal criterion. The statement requires that those intangible assets be recognized as assets apart from goodwill even if confidentiality or other contractual terms prohibit the sale or transfer of the contract separately from the acquired entity.

All customer relationship intangibles with a suggestion of a contractual relationship are included in these data. Categories include customer contracts, customer relationships with contracts, customer contracts and relationships, contract backlog (distinguished from order backlog), etc. In just over 9% of the PPAs observed for this section, a range of values for remaining useful life were used. Ranges were averaged for purposes of these data when the weighted average was not specified.

Customer Contracts Benchmarks and Remaining Useful Lives

Customer Contracts			
Useful Life		**Value as Percentage of Total Intangible Assets**	
# Observations:	61	# Observations:	155
Average:	6.2 years	Average:	21.0%
25th percentile:	3.0 years	25th percentile:	5.2%
Median:	6.0 years	Median:	12.9%
75th percentile:	8.0 years	75th percentile:	25.6%
Mode:	1.0 years		
Value as Percentage of Identifiable Intangible Assets		**Value as Percentage of Business Selling Price**	
# Observations:	155	# Observations:	156
Average:	43.9%	Average:	19.5%
25th percentile:	15.1%	25th percentile:	4.9%
Median:	32.3%	Median:	10.6%
75th percentile:	76.1%	75th percentile:	22.0%

Notes:

- For readers interested in distribution contracts, one observation identified this intangible and assigned a remaining useful life of five years; and
- The criterion for including customer contracts as an identifiable asset is different from that allowing inclusion of customer relationships. Accordingly, most analysts separate customer relationships from contracts, and that data proved to support the decision to keep them separate (see following section).

Customer Relationships

If a customer relationship does not arise from a contract, the FASB statement requires that it be recognized as an intangible asset apart from goodwill if it meets the separability criterion. Exchange transactions for the same asset or a similar type of asset provide evidence of separability of a noncontractual customer relationship and might also provide information about exchange prices that should be considered when estimating its fair value. For example, relationships with depositors are frequently exchanged with the related deposits and, thus, meet the criteria for recognition as an intangible asset apart from goodwill.

Whereas, for B2C companies, intangible assets are often dominated by brand value, for many B2B companies, they are a set of relationships with a core group of powerful customers. When these relationships are well developed and ongoing, they produce sustainable returns to shareholders. Commercial customer relationship value represents the largest intangible asset (aside from goodwill) identified in the purchase price allocations studied for this analysis.

The value of a customer relationship reflects the present value of future incomes from that relationship, and the value reflected in a purchase price allocation should reconcile to the sum of all of the values of individual customer relationships held by an acquired company, though it would be prohibitively expensive to perform such a proof.

Factors to Consider

In his 2007 paper "What Drives Customer Relationship Value in Business-to-Business Exchanges?" Robert W. Palmatier posits that, from the company perspective, value drivers are longevity of seller contacts, industry dynamism, and the history of new product launches.

Gustavo Bermejo et al., of Madrid Technological University, attempting to be more precise in defining and clarifying the relationships among the concepts of customer equity (CE), lifetime value (LTV), and customer relationship management (CRM), concluded LTV is the best financial outcome to measure customer value.

Bermejo focused on the business-to-business market, but his research translates to other markets. He identified key valuation factors that impact customer relationships: expected income stream, the sustainability of any competitive advantage, market share and position, and the causal relationship between marketing actions and customer reactions. Though terms are different, Palmatier and Bermejo's findings are remarkably similar.

What Palmatier lumps into "history of new product launches" can easily be parsed into customer relationship management expertise within a subject company. And measurement of that expertise leads to a customer equity value, a method of valuing a whole base of customers. As stated above, the determination of CE is the sum of the LTVs for each customer: Bermejo defines LTV as the net present value of a single customer's income stream and CE as the discounted sum of the LTVs. Customer relationship management theory ties directly to valuation, as customers, though they are intangibles, should be managed as assets, and management should allow for maximization of the total base, not just one set or one customer.

CE incorporates retention experience and an organization's up- and cross-selling experience. And, though it is a financial metric, it is not independent. For example, Rust et al. (2000) discuss how customers' feelings about a company's brand affects their loyalty. What are the customer's perceptions and expectations about price, quality, and service? The higher the degree of satisfaction, and the higher the expectations, the stronger is the basis for a long-term, customer relationship.

In a business-to-business setting (with fewer customers, each being more important than in a typical B2C setting), as outlined by Stahl et al. in 2003, a valuation model or the derivation of customer equity would incorporate four estimates, the last one of which is seldom quantified:

1. Cash flow from products and services that form the basis of the customer relationship;
2. Cash flow from up- and cross-selling and increases in market share;
3. Cash flow from customer referrals; and
4. Cash flow resulting from learning that takes place as a direct result of a customer relationship.

Cash flow models take costs into account and, therefore, help sift through the myth (based on Pareto's Law) that the largest customers are always the most profitable. Larger companies may demand significant discounts; smaller companies may demand proportionally greater service. Costs to be taken into account include advertising and promotion, customer service, and customer retention (keep in mind that customer relationships expected to be added in the future and the related costs are typically not included in a valuation).

Risk

Stahl also cautions valuators on the impact of a longer time horizon for a customer relationship. The longer the time horizon, the more purchase cycles are incorporated, with each one having a given probability of reaching a successful conclusion. Multiplying probable outcomes together yields greater uncertainty, increasing the cost of capital and requiring application of a higher discount rate.

At the industry level, vulnerability and volatility of cash flows is influenced by competitive forces, growth rates, mergers and acquisitions, market entry barriers, substitution threats, etc. At the company level, quality of management, investment decisions, the nature and stability of customer-supplier relationships, CRM capabilities, management insights about competition and customer defection rates, etc., affect uncertainty.

Ryals and Knox developed a "relationship risk scorecard" in 2007 that can be used as a risk checklist for valuing customer relationships, one by one.

1. *Overall relationship, including how long the relationship has been in place, how many contacts have been developed with the customer, and how many different product lines are purchased by the customer.* Deloitte analysts refer to the same phenomenon this way: High-value customer relationships will typically experience a type of inertia, meaning it is easier for them to remain customers than migrate. (Today this is referred to as "stickiness," and it may be because of pricing advantages, brand, or a multitude of things.)

   P.J. Patel, CFA, ASA, and Ed Hamilton, CFA, wrote in *Business Valuation Update* about the distributor method to value customer relationships, as a modification to the multiperiod excess earnings method. MPEEM requires significant market evidence; especially at the asset level, where it may be challenging to find royalty indications that are directly comparable to the asset being valued. In certain industries and situations, this framework, given limitations on the availability of data, may be highly subjective and, if applied in a mechanical manner, may provide a value conclusion that is inconsistent with a qualitative assessment of the entity and its underlying assets. To address these limitations and reduce subjectivity when valuing customer-related assets, in certain situations, we began replacing the company-specific margin (or PFI) with a market-based margin, as a reasonable market proxy, in an MPEEM. This method is commonly referred to as the distributor method. The name is derived from the initial use of distribution companies as the market proxy.

2. *Extent of knowledge of the customer, including the customer's industry.* Typically, if a company monitors customer purchases, payments, trends, complaints, and intercompany contacts, the value of the customer relationships will be greater. The more known about a customer, the more accurately can be assessed the risks associated with each and the collective risks (and remedies) associated with the customer equity, or the value of the whole of customer relationships.

That is not to say that a longer useful life ultimately works against an entity. All things being equal, the customer relationships intangible asset with a longer expected remaining useful life is more valuable than an identical asset with a shorter remaining useful life, regardless of valuation approach employed.

Useful Life

Commercial customer relationships are typically considered a wasting asset. Since the customer equity is the sum total of the individual customer relationships valued, the expected remaining useful life of the asset is that period from the date of valuation to when the last customer relationship is expected to end.

The first item of analysis of customer relationships is an examination of their nature. Are the relationships similar with respect to revenue and profitability expectations? Do they have similar expected remaining useful lives? If they do, valuators can use attrition analysis to estimate useful lives (e.g., the revenue and profitability for the customer equity in future years will be a function of what it was in the previous year. This exponential distribution is different from what we see in the analysis of purchase price allocations, as straight line is the preferred amortization method.)

If the individual customer relationships display unique characteristics (revenue, profitability, expected remaining useful life), then a "more rigorous survivor curve method" should be considered. (A thorough analysis of methods of determining remaining useful lives is found in Pamela Garland's article "Existing Intellectual Property Remaining Useful Life" in the 2004 special edition of Willamette Management Associates' *Insights*.)

It is likely valuation analysts will find a hybrid customer relationships asset, with groups of homogenous customer types, each one lending itself to its own, distinct attrition analysis. More complicated is the situation combining homogeneous customer groups with those that defy lumping into similar revenue, profitability, or remaining useful life categories.

Customer Relationships Benchmarks and Remaining Useful Lives

Customer Relationships			
Useful Life		**Value as Percentage of Total Intangible Assets**	
# Observations:	371	# Observations:	828
# Indefinite:	1		
# Amortized:	370	Average:	23.7%
Average:	10.0 years	25th percentile:	7.9%
25th percentile:	6.0 years	Median:	18.2%
Median:	9.5 years	75th percentile:	31.8%
75th percentile:	12.5 years		
Mode:	10.0 years	**Value as Percentage of Business Selling Price**	
Value as Percentage of Identifiable Intangible Assets		# Observations:	837
# Observations:	828	Average:	20.2%
		25th percentile:	6.5%
Average:	52.9%	Median:	14.8%
25th percentile:	24.0%	75th percentile:	27.5%
Median:	46.7%		
75th percentile:	72.7%		

Notes:

- Several observations included multiple listings for customer relationships when each could be segregated and assigned distinct useful lives:
  - One observation distinguished between channel relationships (three years) and customer relationships (two years); two PPAs distinguished between distributor relationships (10 and 12 years) and customer relationships (two and 12 years);
  - Nine PPAs distinguished between distributor relationships and customer relationships. Of those nine, three listed a useful life for distributor relationships (10, 12, and 13 years) and three listed a useful life for customer relationships (two, two, and 12 years);
  - One PPA separated national accounts (20 years) from other customer relationships (six years);
  - One observation distinguished between global relationships (indefinite remaining useful life), European relationships (eight years), and U.S. relationships (10 years); and
  - Two observations separated maintenance relationships from product relationships. Only one assigned useful lives, assigning 6.6 years to maintenance relationships and 4.3 years to product relationships.
- For purposes of this study, "customer relationships" includes several references to customer base;
- Vendor relationships as a category was not included in customer relationships;
- Straight-line method depreciation is the default choice, though most filers don't specify. One observation described using estimated attrition; and
- One PPA chose indefinite for the remaining useful life of customer relationships. This was not included in the mean and median calculations.

Order Backlog

Order backlog consists of noncontracted-for, unfunded orders in a pipeline. These orders will either come in soon or require more assistance to secure, assistance not taken into account in a valuation. They are to be distinguished from contracted sales or funded sales, and many times get assigned a remaining useful life of a partial year.

Order Backlog Benchmarks and Remaining Useful Lives

Order Backlog			
Useful Life		**Value as Percentage of Total Intangible Assets**	
# Observations:	67	# Observations:	123
Average:	1.5 years	Average:	3.9%
25th percentile:	0.5 years	25th percentile:	0.7%
Median:	1.0 years	Median:	1.6%
75th percentile:	2.0 years	75th percentile:	4.0%
Mode:	1.0 years		
Value as Percentage of Identifiable Intangible Assets		**Value as Percentage of Business Selling Price**	
# Observations:	128	# Observations:	123
Average:	8.2%	Average:	2.7%
25th percentile:	1.5%	25th percentile:	0.5%
Median:	3.6%	Median:	1.3%
75th percentile:	10.1%	75th percentile:	3.4%

Sales (Customer) Contract Backlog

Sales contracts are contrasted with orders in that they are either funded or enforceable by law, mostly over a longer time period, resulting in longer RULs.

Sales (Customer) Contract Backlog Benchmarks and Remaining Useful Lives

Sales (Customer) Contract Backlog			
Useful Life		**Value as Percentage of Total Intangible Assets**	
# Observations:	14	# Observations:	22
Average:	2.6 years	Average:	3.8%
25th percentile:	1.0 years	25th percentile:	1.2%
Median:	1.5 years	Median:	2.2%
75th percentile:	3.0 years	75th percentile:	6.0%
Mode:	1.0 years		
Value as Percentage of Identifiable Intangible Assets		**Value as Percentage of Business Selling Price**	
# Observations:	22	# Observations:	22
Average:	11.7%	Average:	2.7%
25th percentile:	4.4%	25th percentile:	1.0%
Median:	7.4%	Median:	1.7%
75th percentile:	14.7%	75th percentile:	3.6%

Chapter 6. Favorable Contracts (Not Sales)

Favorable contracts are identifiable intangible assets. An example given in the FASB Statement is of an acquired entity operating a manufacturing facility under a lease that has terms quite favorable relative to market prices. In the example, the lease terms explicitly prohibit transfer of the lease (through either sale or sublease). In this case, the value arising from that operating lease contract is an intangible asset that meets the contractual-legal criterion for recognition apart from goodwill, even though the lease contract cannot be sold or otherwise transferred.

Here's a second example offered in the statement: An acquired entity owns and operates a nuclear power plant. The license to operate that power plant is an intangible asset that meets the contractual-legal criterion for recognition apart from goodwill, even if it cannot be sold or transferred apart from the acquired power plant. Importantly, the statement does not preclude an acquiring entity from recognizing the fair value of the operating license and the fair value of the power plant as a single asset for financial reporting purposes if the useful lives of those assets are similar.

At an Illinois NACVA chapter meeting in 2009, Robert Reilly of Willamette Management Associates listed the types of assets that might make up the contracts category:

1. Licensing, royalty, and standstill agreements;
2. Advertising, construction, management, and service or supply contracts;
3. Lease agreements;
4. Construction permits;
5. Franchise agreements;
6. Operating and broadcast rights;
7. Use rights such as drilling, water, air, mineral, timber cutting, and route authorities;
8. Servicing contracts such as mortgage servicing contracts; and
9. Employment contracts.

Valuation of a favorable contract values that part of the contract that is favorable, that which is better than market rates. What makes it an identifiable intangible asset is the fact that it is favorable.

Though an analyst should still consider how all of the useful life criteria might affect the contract (legal life, contractual life, physical/functional life, technological life, economic life, and analytical life), contractual life is the most relied upon criterion with respect to remaining useful lives of favorable contracts.

Favorable Contracts Benchmarks and Remaining Useful Lives

Favorable Contracts

Useful Life

# Observations:	81
# Indefinite:	5
# Amortized:	76
Average:	10.4 years
25th percentile:	3.4 years
Median:	6.8 years
75th percentile:	12.3 years
Mode:	5.0 years

Value as Percentage of Identifiable Intangible Assets

# Observations:	261
Average:	26.6%
25th percentile:	5.0%
Median:	17.7%
75th percentile:	46.9%

Value as Percentage of Total Intangible Assets

# Observations:	379
Average:	24.3%
25th percentile:	3.2%
Median:	14.9%
75th percentile:	34.9%

Value as Percentage of Business Selling Price

# Observations:	398
Average:	18.5%
25th percentile:	2.6%
Median:	10.2%
75th percentile:	25.4%

Note:

- One hundred twenty-two observations had a value for favorable contracts that comprised greater than 80% of the total value of the identifiable intangibles for the firm. These agreements were not included when looking at the value percentages.
- The five items that were given an indefinite life were listed as "management contract," "FCC license," "certificates of need," "lender's license," and "accreditations and designations."

Chapter 7. Noncompetes

In the February 2012 issue of BVR's *Business Valuation Update,* Gary Trugman outlined an approach to valuing noncompete agreements.

The most common approach to valuing a covenant not-to-compete involves a "with and without" analysis, in which the appraiser estimates value based on the difference of two discounted future benefits calculations. A similar method, the lost profits analysis, which projects the present value profits that the acquired company would lose if the seller continued to compete, will reach pretty much the same value. A third method, compensation-based, measures the income that the seller loses due to the covenant not-to compete (CNC), but it is not always appropriate since it does not measure value to the purchasing party. A CNC is an agreement between parties to the sale of a business by which the seller typically agrees not to compete in the same industry for a specified period of time and within a specific geographic period. A CNC can be part of a large corporate asset sale or divestiture, or it can accompany the sale of a solo professional practice or family business. In either case, the contract for sale may include the covenants, or they can appear in a separate, noncompete agreement.

In most cases, an eight-step approach, "with and without," will provide a comprehensive and correct method for valuing the noncompete. Except for the last two, it's not a requirement that these steps occur in sequence:

1. Identify the legitimacy and "economic reality" of the noncompete (explained in more detail below);

2. Determine the value of the company assuming enforcement of the CNC. The parties may have already allocated this value in their agreements or in forecasts used to determine acquisition price.

3. Develop projections assuming competition from the selling party based on historical trends and margins, growth drivers, asset utilization ratios, capital expenditures, etc.;

4. Determine the overall value of the company assuming competition from the seller, using the forecasts developed in Step 3;

5. Determine the differential between the values derived in Steps 2 and 4;

6. Quantify the impact of amortization (tax savings) depending on the purpose and function of the valuation. In effect, once you have valued the CNC, do another projection that uses the deductibility of the CNC amortization to adjust the future taxable income (and thus profits);

7. Calculate the final value of the CNC, with any additional adjustments based on the probability of the seller's competition; and

8. Conduct a "sanity check." Does the concluded value make sense, taking into consideration the bigger picture of the business, industry, and other economic factors?

Obviously, the value of a noncompete cannot exceed the total purchase price. Analysts can also check for reasonableness by examining the percentage of noncompete value to total transaction values of other comparable sales.

Economic Reality

How does one determine the legitimacy of a noncompete agreement? (Keep in mind that legitimacy does not equate to legal enforceability, which requires the opinion of legal counsel.) Several court cases have developed tests by which to determine the "economic reality" of noncompete agreements. For instance, in *Forward Communications Corp. v. United States*, 608 F.2d 485 (Ct. Cl. 1979), the Federal Court of Claims summarized the four conditions that a noncompete should meet to qualify for federal tax amortization:

- *Severability.* Is the compensation paid for the noncompete agreement severable from the price paid for the acquired goodwill?

- *Anticipated repudiation.* Is either party to the contract attempting to repudiate an amount that they both knowingly fixed or allocated to the noncompete?

- *Intent.* Is there evidence that both parties intended to assign a price to the noncompete when they executed the purchase and sale agreement?

- *Economic reality.* Is the covenant economically real and meaningful?

The facts and circumstances in any individual case are important to consider. The sale documents, agreements, and discussions between the buyer and seller are also vital components to understanding the evolution and import of the deal and whether a covenant to not compete has economic substance and legitimacy.

Following *Forward Communications* and the cases cited therein, the Tax Court set forth an 11-factor test to determine the economic reality of a noncompete in *Thompson v. Commissioner*, T.C. Memo 1996-468 (1996) (available at *BVLaw*, www.businessvaluationlaw.com). These 11 points also furnish a good basis for assessing the probability of the seller's competition:

1. *Grantor's business expertise.* What knowledge and skills are necessary to run a competing business? Does the seller (grantor of the noncompete) have these requisite skills?

2. *Grantor's intent to compete.* Why did the grantor sell the company? Does the grantor intend to return to the market after the CNC expires?

3. *Grantor's economic resources.* Does the grantor have the financial capacity and resources to compete with the acquired company?

4. *Potential damage to the grantee.* Will the acquired company (grantee) lose business if the grantor chooses to compete?

5. *Grantor's network.* Did the grantor build relationships with customers, suppliers, and other contacts of the acquired business? Will customers and suppliers choose to do business with the acquired company or the grantor?

6. *Duration and geographic scope.* Where did the grantor do business prior to the sale of the company? Does the noncompete adequately restrict the grantor from competing in this area?

7. *Enforceability.* Does state law permit the enforcement of the noncompete? Are the consequences for breach as expressly stated in the noncompete agreement legal?

8. *Age and health of the grantor.* Given the age, health, and retirement prospects of the grantor, is it reasonable that he or she will be able to compete with the acquired company?

9. *Payment terms.* How do the sale agreements measure payments to the grantor? If they require payment over the term of the noncompete, and if there is more than one selling shareholder, are those payments pro rata by ownership interest to all shareholders? Is payment measured by contributions to the company prior to acquisition?

10. *Payment duration.* If the sale agreements require payment over the term of the noncompete, what happens to that obligation should the grantor die or breach the contract?

11. *Negotiations.* Did the parties "vigorously" negotiate the terms and value for sale of the company and its assets?

Rob Schlegel at Houlihan Valuation Services in Indianapolis simplifies this list:

1. Does the departing owner desire to stay in this business in this location? (Desirability)

2. Now that the existing business has been sold and the departing owner no longer has access to those assets, does the departing owner have the capacity to compete? (Capacity)

3. Does the departing owner have the ability (time, resources, etc.) to compete? (Ability)

Noncompetes Benchmarks and Remaining Useful Lives

Noncompetes

Useful Life
Observations: 13,216

Average:	4.4 years
25th percentile:	3.0 years
Median:	5.0 years
75th percentile:	5.0 years
Mode:	5.0 years

Value as Percentage of Identifiable Intangible Assets
Observations: 669

Average:	24.5%
25th percentile:	3.1%
Median:	12.1%
75th percentile:	45.2%

Value as Percentage of Total Intangible Assets
Observations: 2,523

Average:	19.2%
25th percentile:	2.9%
Median:	10.0%
75th percentile:	29.6%

Value as Percentage of Business Selling Price
Observations: 2,925

Average:	11.1%
25th percentile:	2.0%
Median:	5.9%
75th percentile:	15.6%

Notes:

- There were 612 PPAs where noncompete agreements were the sole identifiable intangible asset. These agreements were not included when looking at the value percentages of noncompetes to identifiable intangible assets.
- Particularly helpful to analysts requiring more benchmarking information on valuing noncompetes is the section on industry data slices.

Chapter 8. Indefinite-Lived Intangibles

GOODWILL

Goodwill represents the excess of the aggregate purchase price over the fair value of net assets, including IPR&D, of an acquired business. Goodwill is tested for impairment annually, more frequently if changes in circumstance or the occurrence of events suggest impairment exists. The test for impairment requires several estimates about fair value, most of which are based on projected future cash flows.

In a 2009 article in the *CPA Journal,* Ronald Huefner and James Largay III gave background information for the need for SFAS 141, *Business Combinations,* and SFAS 142, *Goodwill and Other Intangible Assets.* SFAS 141 eliminated the pooling-of-interests method of accounting for business combinations, a method that avoided the goodwill issue entirely.

SFAS 142 made two major changes to goodwill accounting:

- Amortization of *all* goodwill ceased, regardless of when it originated. Goodwill is now carried as an asset without reduction for periodic amortization; and
- Companies are to assess goodwill for impairment at least annually. If goodwill is impaired, its carrying amount is reduced and an impairment loss is recognized.

Companies were required to implement these new standards in fiscal years beginning after Dec. 15, 2001, with early adoption permitted for fiscal years beginning after March 31, 2001. During the first six months following adoption of SFAS 142, companies assessed existing goodwill balances for impairment and reported any such transitional impairment losses as due to a change in accounting principle.

Goodwill Benchmarks and Remaining Useful Lives

Goodwill

Useful Life

# Observations:	4,480
Average:	Indefinite
Median:	Indefinite
Mode:	Indefinite

Goodwill - All Transactions

Value as Percentage of Total Intangible Assets

# Observations:	4,251
Average:	69.9%
25th percentile:	50.0%
Median:	73.3%
75th percentile:	98.8%

Value as Percentage of Business Selling Price

# Observations:	4,480
Average:	64.3%
25th percentile:	29.1%
Median:	50.6%
75th percentile:	72.4%

Goodwill - Companies Sold for <$5 Million

Value as Percentage of Total Intangible Assets

# Observations:	1,975
Average:	80.9%
25th percentile:	64.9%
Median:	97.0%
75th percentile:	100.0%

Value as Percentage of Business Selling Price

# Observations:	2,067
Average:	54.6%
25th percentile:	27.8%
Median:	54.5%
75th percentile:	79.5%

Goodwill - Companies Sold for >$5 Million

Value as Percentage of Total Intangible Assets

# Observations:	2,279
Average:	60.3%
25th Percentile:	44.0%
Median:	62.0%
75th Percentile	78.4%

Value as Percentage of Business Selling Price

# Observations:	2,416
Average:	72.6%
25th percentile:	30.0%
Median:	48.8%
75th percentile:	66.7%

Note:

- Four of the purchase price allocations amortized goodwill. Two purchase price allocations amortized goodwill for three years (both transactions occurred in the year 2000), one amortized goodwill for 10 years (the transaction occurred in 2000), and one amortized goodwill for 15 years (the transaction occurred in 1999). All the amortizations were on a straight-line basis.
- The statistics above only include purchase price allocations where goodwill was listed in the purchase price allocation.

ASSEMBLED WORKFORCE

The most common type of human capital intangible is a business unit's trained and assembled workforce. The assembled workforce intangible asset is the employer's expectation that experienced employees will report to work tomorrow morning. The employer also expects that these employees:

1. Are trained in how to perform their duties and responsibilities;
2. Know how to operate any equipment for which they are responsible;
3. Are knowledgeable of the goals and protocols of the subject organization; and
4. Are experienced working with and communicating with each other.

It used to be that assembled workforce was valued separately from goodwill. Now, even though some preparers of purchase price allocations extract it, it is considered part of goodwill. In valuing an assembled workforce, i.e., in-place management, an established sales team, MIS, etc., a cost savings approach is typically employed. Consideration is given to classified advertising, agency fees, reimbursed applicant expenses, relocation expenses, corporate recruiting and training staff compensation, etc.

Assembled Workforce Benchmarks and Remaining Useful Lives

Assembled Workforce			
Value as Percentage of Total Intangible Assets		**Value as Percentage of Goodwill Value (transactions where both goodwill and assembled workforce were separately identified)**	
# Observations:	71	# Observations:	66
Average:	6.3%	Average:	17.7%
25th percentile:	1.1%	25th percentile:	1.5%
Median:	2.5%	Median:	3.5%
75th percentile:	5.6%	75th percentile:	12.6%
Value as Percentage of Business Selling Price			
# Observations:	72		
Average:	5.4%		
25th percentile:	1.1%		
Median:	2.4%		
75th percentile:	5.9%		

Notes:

- Mode remaining useful life: Indefinite
- Only four of the purchase price allocations amortized the assembled workforce intangible. One purchase price allocation assigned assembled workforce a one-year useful life, while the other three assigned a three-year useful life.
- Assembled workforce is now considered part of goodwill, and most purchase price allocations do not segregate the two.

IPR&D (IN PROCESS RESEARCH & DEVELOPMENT)

An acquirer is required to recognize all tangible and intangible assets acquired in a business combination that are to be used in research and development (R&D) activities regardless of whether these assets have an alternative future use by the acquirer. FASB ASC 350-30 requires that these assets be classified as indefinite-lived until the completion or abandonment of the associated R&D efforts, at which time the entity would determine the assets' appropriate useful life.

In the new valuation guide to IPR&D, the AICPA defines the relationship between R&D projects and R&D assets: "In this guide, an R&D project that has not yet been completed is referred to as an *IPR&D project.* Intangible assets that are to be used or are used in R&D activities, including specific IPR&D projects, are referred to as *IPR&D assets.* In other words, an IPR&D project is an example of an IPR&D asset. However, in some cases, an IPR&D project may comprise several IPR&D assets. In this chapter, unless indicated otherwise, the term *IPR&D asset* refers to an IPR&D asset acquired in a business combination." The guide divides such assets into four categories:

1. R&D efforts of acquiree to be continued by the acquirer;
2. Defensive:

   "If the reporting entity intends to lock up an acquired intangible asset to prevent others from obtaining access to the asset in order to 'defend' the value of other intangible assets used in R&D activities, the task force believes that such asset would be considered 'used in R&D activities.'"
3. Outlicensing arrangements with active involvement (the key is "active involvement, as the task force that developed the guide believes if the acquirer intends to outlicense an acquired intangible but does NOT plan to be actively involved in its development, that asset would not be 'used in R&D activities.'"); and
4. Temporarily idled assets.

Valuation Approaches

When valuing an IPR&D asset, cost, market and income approaches each should be considered.

FASB ASC 820-10-35-24 states that a "reporting entity shall use valuation techniques that are appropriate in the circumstances and for which sufficient data are available to measure fair value, maximizing the use of relevant observable inputs and minimizing the use of unobservable inputs."

Typically the income approach is used, and the most common methods and techniques employed are:

- Multiperiod excess earnings;
- Relief from royalty;
- Decision tree analysis; and
- "Split" methods (that is, revenue, cash flows, or profit split).

Other methods and techniques under the income approach listed in the guide are:

- Monte Carlo analysis;
- Options-based methods;
- Manufacturing cost savings;
- Incremental revenue or profit (for example, price premium);
- "With and without" analysis; and
- Greenfield method.

The stream of cash flows from each of these methods is discounted to present value, including, as appropriate, any tax benefits derived from amortizing the intangible asset for tax purposes, to estimate the fair value of the intangible asset.

Rule of Thumb for Remaining Useful Lives

In general, the guide asks valuators to look at "incompleteness" as an essential characteristic of IPR&D assets, so much so that "intangible assets used in R&D lacking that characteristic (that is, assets that are complete) that are being used the way they are intended to be used would not be considered IPR&D assets and should be accounted for in accordance with their nature; whereas intangible assets that are incomplete and used in R&D activities should be accounted for in accordance with FASB ASC 350-30-35-17A (that is, assigned an indefinite useful life upon acquisition)."

Notwithstanding the above, the guide allows for some exceptions:

> To the extent that individually completed intangible assets are solely and directly related to IPR&D projects that are still in development (for example, in the pharmaceutical industry, a patent on a compound that has not yet been approved), such assets may be aggregated with other intangible assets used in R&D activities. That is, an acquirer would recognize one asset for each IPR&D project, which would comprise all the intangible assets used exclusively in that project, and that asset would be assigned an indefinite useful life.

IPR&D Benchmarks and Remaining Useful Lives

IPR&D

Useful Life	
# Observations:	32
# Expensed/Written-off	11
# Amortized:	12
(of those amortized)	
Average:	7.7 years
25th percentile:	5.0 years
Median:	7.0 years
75th percentile:	10.0 years
Value as Percentage of Identifiable Intangible Assets	
# Observations:	429
Average:	34.0%
25th percentile:	6.5%
Median:	17.7%
75th percentile:	54.7%
Value as Percentage of Total Intangible Assets	
# Observations:	429
Average:	20.4%
25th percentile:	2.3%
Median:	7.3%
75th percentile:	28.4%
Value as Percentage of Business Selling Price	
# Observations:	435
Average:	30.0%
25th percentile:	2.1%
Median:	5.9%
75th percentile:	25.0%

Notes:

- Mode remaining useful life: Indefinite
- Only 12 of the purchase price allocations amortized IPR&D, and 11 expensed/wrote off IPR&D.

Chapter 9. Data Slices: By Identifiable Intangible Asset Category

Useful Lives (Years)					
	Average	25th P	Median	75th P	# Observations
Patents	8.3	5.0	7.0	10.0	46
Software	5.6	3.0	5.0	7.4	54
Technology	7.1	5.0	6.0	9.2	271
Databases	10.1	5.9	10.0	11.0	22
Trade Secrets	8.3	4.0	5.0	8.0	11
Trademarks	9.3	4.0	7.0	13.0	75
Trade Names	7.9	3.0	5.0	10.0	189
Trademarks and Trade Names	8.9	5.0	8.5	10.0	90
Copyrights	*	*	*	*	*
Domains	*	*	*	*	*
Customer Lists	10.6	5.0	10.0	17.0	30
Customer Contracts	6.2	3.0	6.0	8.0	61
Customer Relationships	10.0	6.0	9.5	12.5	371
Order Backlog	1.5	0.5	1.0	2.0	67
Contract Backlog	2.6	1.0	1.5	3.0	14
Favorable Contracts	10.4	3.4	6.8	12.3	81
Noncompetes	4.4	3.0	5.0	5.0	13,216
Goodwill	Indef		Indef		4,480
Workforce	Indef		Indef		72
IPR&D	Indef		Indef		435

* There were a limited number of observations for these intangible asset classes. Please refer to their individual sections for more detailed information.

Value as Percentage of Identifiable Intangible Assets					
	Average	25th P	Median	75th P	# Observations
Patents	35.2%	6.3%	18.6%	58.3%	121
Software	37.7%	7.1%	25.3%	63.1%	152
Technology	44.6%	24.0%	43.5%	63.5%	620
Databases	36.5%	7.4%	36.8%	53.1%	40
Trade Secrets	33.4%	9.4%	26.1%	46.1%	32
Trademarks	25.0%	4.3%	10.9%	32.3%	176
Trade Names	23.1%	4.3%	14.1%	36.2%	472
Trademarks and Trade Names	22.9%	1.6%	6.0%	16.7%	219
Copyrights	*	*	*	*	*
Domains	38.8%	2.0%	21.7%	82.6%	35
Customer Lists	56.7%	26.0%	51.2%	94.8%	176
Customer Contracts	49.2%	15.1%	32.3%	76.1%	155
Customer Relationships	52.9%	24.0%	46.7%	72.7%	828
Order Backlog	8.2%	1.5%	3.6%	10.1%	128
Contract Backlog	11.7%	4.4%	7.4%	14.7%	22
Favorable Contracts	26.6%	5.0%	17.7%	46.9%	261
Noncompetes	24.5%	3.1%	12.1%	45.2%	669
Goodwill	N/A	N/A	N/A	N/A	N/A
Workforce	N/A	N/A	N/A	N/A	N/A
IPR&D	N/A	N/A	N/A	N/A	N/A

* There were a limited number of observations for these intangible asset classes.
Please refer to their individual sections for more detailed information.
N/A = Not Available.

Value as Percentage of Total Intangible Assets					
	Average	25th P	Median	75th P	# Observations
Patents	19.1%	1.6%	7.1%	23.3%	121
Software	18.4%	2.4%	9.1%	24.6%	151
Technology	21.2%	7.9%	16.0%	29.4%	618
Databases	18.2%	2.9%	9.1%	22.0%	39
Trade Secrets	16.3%	5.0%	11.8%	22.2%	32
Trademarks	15.1%	1.7%	4.6%	14.9%	174
Trade Name	11.4%	1.6%	6.0%	16.7%	472
Trademarks and Trade Names	10.6%	1.7%	5.2%	12.3%	218
Copyrights	*	*	*	*	*
Domain	18.0%	0.8%	4.3%	27.3%	35
Customer Lists	30.9%	8.0%	20.0%	46.3%	176
Customer Contracts	21.0%	5.2%	12.9%	25.6%	155
Customer Relationships	23.7%	7.9%	18.2%	31.8%	828
Order Backlog	3.9%	0.7%	1.6%	4.0%	123
Contract Backlog	3.8%	1.2%	2.2%	6.0%	22
Favorable Contracts	24.3%	3.2%	14.9%	34.9%	379
Noncompetes	19.2%	2.9%	10.0%	29.6%	2,523
Goodwill - All	69.9%	50.0%	73.3%	98.8%	4,251
Goodwill - Sell Price <$5 Mil	80.9%	64.9%	97.0%	100.0%	1,975
Goodwill - Sell Price >$5 Mil	60.3%	44.0%	62.0%	78.4%	2,279
Workforce	6.3%	1.1%	2.5%	5.6%	71
IPR&D	20.4%	2.3%	7.3%	28.4%	429

* There were a limited number of observations for this intangible asset class.
Please refer to the individual section for more detailed information.

Chapter 10. Data Slices: By Industry

This section presents data organized by intangible type and industry. The initial charts provide data on an average basis, followed by charts providing data on a median basis. The remaining useful lives are provided by intangible type and industry, and the value of the intangible—relative to identifiable intangibles, total intangibles, and business selling price—is also provided for each industry.

The count of purchase price allocations is provided for each industry. This figure does not necessarily reflect the number of observations for each intangible asset class in the summary information.

Average Intangible Life (years)											
Industry	NAICS	Total # of Observations*	Patents	Software	Databases	Technology	Trade Secrets	Trademarks (when amortized)	Trademarks (# of indefinites)	Trade Names	Trade Names (# of indefinites)
Agriculture, Forestry, Fishing and Hunting	11	7									
Mining, Quarrying, and Oil and Gas Extraction	21	79		5.0 years						40.0 years	1
Utilities	22	25								10.0 years	
Construction	23	119							1	9.5 years	2
Manufacturing	31 - 33	1,432	9.1 years	7.7 years	18.0 years	8.3 years	5.4 years	11.0 years	12	8.3 years	25
Pharmaceuticals	325412	177	10.7 years			11.6 years		13.0 years		8.4 years	
Wholesale Trade	42	271	9.7 years			7.8 years	6.0 years	6.5 years	2	10.7 years	2
Retail Trade	44 - 45	711				4.0 years				8.6 years	3
Transportation and Warehousing	48 - 49	156				15.0 years					1
Information	51	664	4.9 years	5.8 years	7.5 years	5.4 years	3.0 years	5.4 years		5.9 years	5
Software	511210	381	4.6 years	6.2 years	6.6 years	5.4 years	3.0 years	5.1 years		5.5 years	
Technology	511210, 518210, 541511, 541512	583	4.7 years	5.8 years	6.6 years	5.7 years	3.0 years	5.8 years		5.6 years	
Finance and Insurance	52	260		3.3 years		5.7 years		17.5 years		7.8 years	4
Real Estate and Rental and Leasing	53	132	6.5 years	3.0 years	6.0 years	7.0 years		5.0 years	2	13.0 years	
Professional, Scientific, and Technical Services	54	467	10.5 years	5.9 years	8.0 years	7.3 years	5.5 years	11.0 years	1	5.3 years	2
Consulting	541330, 541612, 541613, 541614, 541618, 541690	112		6.0 years	10.0 years	5.8 years	6.0 years			3.9 years	
Management of Companies and Enterprises	55	56		5.0 years		20.0 years				15.8 years	
Administrative and Support and Waste Management and Remediation Services	56	413		4.3 years	18.8 years	6.8 years	35.0 years	15.0 years	1	9.4 years	5
Educational Services	61	52					5.0 years		1	15.0 years	1
Health Care and Social Assistance	62	260	5.0 years			8.2 years		8.0 years	1	5.0 years	1
Arts, Entertainment, and Recreation	71	69									
Accommodation and Food Services	72	659							1		
Other Services (except Public Administration)	81	492			10.0 years	3.3 years	10.0 years	15.0 years		10.0 years	1
All Industries	11 - 81	6,329	8.3 years	5.6 years	10.1 years	7.1 years	8.3 years	9.3 years	22	7.9 years	53

* The total number of observations is the total number of purchase price allocations for each industry. The figure does not necessarily reflect the number of observations for each intangible asset class in the summary information. The count of observations excludes those for noncompetes; there were over 13,000 observations of noncompete lives and values.
The purchase price allocations are organized by sector, according to the North American Industry Classification System. For more information, visit www.census.gov.

Average Intangible Life (years), continued												
Industry	Trademarks and Trade Names	Trademarks and Trade Names (# of indefinites)	Domains	Customer Lists	Customer Contracts	Customer Relationships	Order Backlog	Favorable Contracts	Noncompetes	IPR&D (when amortized)	IPR&D (# of indefinites)	IPR&D (# of expensed)
Agriculture, Forestry, Fishing and Hunting									5.0 years			
Mining, Quarrying, and Oil and Gas Extraction						15.0 years		3.0 years	3.8 years			
Utilities						11.8 years		1.5 years	5.0 years			
Construction					3.3 years	9.9 years	5.1 years	15.5 years	4.6 years			
Manufacturing	9.4 years	10		11.9 years	7.5 years	10.6 years	1.1 years	6.5 years	4.5 years	7.9 years	6	6
Pharmaceuticals	10.2 years				12.0 years	11.0 years	1.5 years	11.2 years	3.6 years			
Wholesale Trade		1		17.0 years	4.0 years	11.2 years	0.4 years	6.0 years	4.4 years			
Retail Trade	3.2 years			7.3 years	15.0 years	10.1 years		16.4 years	4.6 years			
Transportation and Warehousing						13.5 years	0.1 years	16.0 years	4.6 years			
Information	9.1 years	2	6.5 years	10.2 years	5.9 years	7.8 years	2.3 years	10.1 years	3.7 years	7.0 years	1	4
Software	8.4 years		3.0 years	12.0 years	5.7 years	7.7 years	2.5 years	6.7 years	3.6 years	7.0 years		
Technology	8.1 years		3.0 years	15.8 years	5.7 years	8.3 years	1.9 years	9.9 years	3.4 years	7.0 years		
Finance and Insurance	5.2 years	1		10.8 years	9.0 years	12.6 years		8.5 years	4.2 years		1	
Real Estate and Rental and Leasing	5.0 years	2			1.0 years	8.3 years		18.0 years	4.6 years			
Professional, Scientific, and Technical Services	7.7 years	2		7.4 years	4.8 years	10.3 years	1.4 years	6.3 years	4.3 years		1	
Consulting	10.0 years			7.0 years	3.8 years	10.7 years	2.1 years	9.0 years	4.4 years			
Management of Companies and Enterprises				18.0 years	8.0 years	16.0 years	3.0 years	23.0 years	2.0 years			
Administrative and Support and Waste Management and Remediation Services	23.3 years	2	19.0 years	3.5 years	5.5 years	12.3 years	5.4 years	27.8 years	4.4 years			1
Educational Services						6.3 years			4.6 years			
Health Care and Social Assistance	10.0 years					9.5 years	3.0 years	10.5 years	3.3 years			
Arts, Entertainment, and Recreation									4.3 years			
Accommodation and Food Services									4.3 years			
Other Services (except Public Administration)	4.0 years			5.0 years	5.0 years	7.4 years		22.5 years	4.5 years			
All Industries	8.9 years	20	10.7 years	10.6 years	6.2 years	10.0 years	1.5 years	10.4 years	4.4 years	7.7 years	9	11

* The total number of observations is the total number of purchase price allocations for each industry. The figure does not necessarily reflect the number of observations for each intangible asset class in the summary information. The count of observations excludes those for noncompetes; there were over 13,000 observations of noncompete lives and values.
The purchase price allocations are organized by sector, according to the North American Industry Classification System. For more information, visit www.census.gov.

Average Intangible Value as a Percentage of Identifiable Intangible Assets									
Industry	NAICS	Total # of Observations*	Patents	Software	Databases	Technology	Trade Secrets	Trademarks	Trade Names
Agriculture, Forestry, Fishing and Hunting	11	7				63.1%			64.4%
Mining, Quarrying, and Oil and Gas Extraction	21	79		1.4%					18.5%
Utilities	22	25							6.0%
Construction	23	119		100.0%		1.1%		12.7%	43.8%
Manufacturing	31 - 33	1,432	35.2%	16.1%	50.3%	47.1%	28.6%	21.5%	19.3%
Pharmaceuticals	325412	177	52.7%	1.0%		52.0%	51.4%	37.5%	10.7%
Wholesale Trade	42	271	34.5%		100.0%	26.5%	50.3%	42.4%	22.6%
Retail Trade	44 - 45	711		76.3%		27.3%		8.3%	48.9%
Transportation and Warehousing	48 - 49	156		16.0%		22.9%	100.0%	6.0%	36.3%
Information	51	664	19.0%	41.6%	34.1%	47.8%	14.4%	8.2%	12.7%
Software	511210	381	20.8%	43.9%	27.5%	49.6%	27.4%	8.1%	8.4%
Technology	511210, 518210, 541511, 541512	583	20.8%	40.0%	35.6%	49.7%	14.4%	7.6%	10.6%
Finance and Insurance	52	260		33.6%		20.3%		10.6%	13.0%
Real Estate and Rental and Leasing	53	132	100.0%	35.4%	30.3%	24.0%		83.3%	48.4%
Professional, Scientific, and Technical Services	54	467	41.7%	32.8%	45.3%	45.1%	34.8%	14.8%	12.8%
Consulting	541330, 541612, 541613, 541614, 541618, 541690	112	2.3%	23.9%	46.6%	25.7%	38.3%		7.6%
Management of Companies and Enterprises	55	56		21.6%		23.5%		91.5%	13.7%
Administrative and Support and Waste Management and Remediation Services	56	413	0.2%	25.9%	23.6%	31.8%	24.8%	34.4%	31.1%
Educational Services	61	52		33.3%	38.5%	61.8%	21.5%	85.0%	40.6%
Health Care and Social Assistance	62	260	1.3%	48.0%	15.9%	29.0%		17.8%	18.9%
Arts, Entertainment, and Recreation	71	69				0.1%	5.1%		25.3%
Accommodation and Food Services	72	659	93.2%				100.0%	86.9%	43.6%
Other Services (except Public Administration)	81	492		90.6%	19.7%	15.5%	17.4%	14.6%	41.3%
All Industries	11 - 81	6,329	35.2%	37.7%	36.5%	44.6%	33.4%	25.0%	23.1%

* The total number of observations is the total number of purchase price allocations for each industry. The figure does not necessarily reflect the number of observations for each intangible asset class in the summary information. The count of observations excludes those for noncompetes; there were over 13,000 observations of noncompete lives and values.
The purchase price allocations are organized by sector, according to the North American Industry Classification System. For more information, visit www.census.gov.

Average Intangible Value as a Percentage of Identifiable Intangible Assets, continued

Industry	Trademarks and Trade Names	Domains	Customer Lists	Customer Contracts	Customer Relationships	Order Backlog	Favorable Contracts	Noncompetes	IPR&D
Agriculture, Forestry, Fishing and Hunting	41.5%				16.5%			3.0%	
Mining, Quarrying, and Oil and Gas Extraction	5.7%				76.5%		5.5%	18.9%	5.0%
Utilities					35.9%		33.3%		
Construction	54.3%		32.1%	25.9%	36.7%	15.0%	32.5%	34.5%	
Manufacturing	26.9%	23.5%	60.1%	35.0%	54.7%	6.4%	18.3%	14.8%	36.7%
Pharmaceuticals	31.4%	0.0%	7.8%	42.6%	38.5%	26.5%	27.8%	8.6%	57.4%
Wholesale Trade	26.8%	48.8%	67.7%	74.7%	60.7%	3.1%	30.5%	18.9%	3.1%
Retail Trade	48.2%	47.5%	49.0%	39.6%	50.6%		38.5%	40.9%	45.5%
Transportation and Warehousing	3.5%	100.0%		62.4%	63.7%	2.5%	27.0%	29.3%	
Information	10.2%	35.2%	48.5%	33.9%	46.5%	8.6%	24.9%	12.2%	22.0%
Software	8.4%	27.7%	36.3%	26.3%	42.0%	8.1%	15.7%	10.1%	20.6%
Technology	9.6%	31.9%	49.8%	31.7%	44.5%	9.5%	18.8%	10.4%	24.4%
Finance and Insurance	23.3%		71.4%	75.4%	59.0%		22.9%	15.8%	0.0%
Real Estate and Rental and Leasing	17.3%	0.5%	69.4%	5.7%	66.8%		12.2%	16.0%	7.0%
Professional, Scientific, and Technical Services	15.6%	12.0%	57.2%	85.5%	55.9%	15.3%	16.6%	14.7%	45.0%
Consulting	12.5%		37.3%	47.7%	64.3%	22.7%	27.2%	20.0%	4.6%
Management of Companies and Enterprises	9.8%		94.6%	51.3%	45.7%	2.7%	34.8%	8.2%	45.6%
Administrative and Support and Waste Management and Remediation Services	12.9%	50.2%	67.9%	65.8%	60.9%	11.1%	35.0%	27.7%	24.8%
Educational Services		4.7%	38.5%	46.5%	27.3%	21.7%	32.7%	20.5%	
Health Care and Social Assistance	25.9%		67.6%	63.8%	55.6%	32.8%	34.8%	19.4%	100.0%
Arts, Entertainment, and Recreation	71.4%		27.3%					51.5%	
Accommodation and Food Services	90.7%		70.0%	43.9%			36.0%	42.5%	
Other Services (except Public Administration)	19.8%	82.4%	40.1%	24.6%	30.2%		47.0%	42.1%	100.0%
All Industries	22.9%	38.8%	56.7%	49.2%	52.9%	8.2%	26.6%	24.5%	34.0%

* The total number of observations is the total number of purchase price allocations for each industry. The figure does not necessarily reflect the number of observations for each intangible asset class in the summary information. The count of observations excludes those for noncompetes; there were over 13,000 observations of noncompete lives and values.
The purchase price allocations are organized by sector, according to the North American Industry Classification System. For more information, visit www.census.gov.

Average Intangible Value as a Percentage of Total Intangible Assets										
Industry	NAICS	Total # of Observations*	Patents	Software	Databases	Technology	Trade Secrets	Trademarks	Trade Names
Agriculture, Forestry, Fishing and Hunting	11	7				47.3%			55.9%
Mining, Quarrying, and Oil and Gas Extraction	21	79		0.5%					6.6%
Utilities	22	25							6.0%
Construction	23	119		8.4%		0.5%		3.7%	19.9%
Manufacturing	31 - 33	1,432	17.2%	9.1%	18.8%	24.3%	12.8%	12.4%	10.5%
Pharmaceuticals	325412	177	35.0%	0.4%		38.0%	17.9%	22.5%	5.5%
Wholesale Trade	42	271	17.8%		86.4%	14.1%	46.5%	25.6%	10.2%
Retail Trade	44 - 45	711		32.7%		9.6%		0.1%	23.9%
Transportation and Warehousing	48 - 49	156		0.6%		7.0%	5.8%	0.9%	12.8%
Information	51	664	6.0%	21.4%	15.5%	20.7%	9.7%	3.0%	4.7%
Software	511210	381	6.0%	22.0%	10.1%	21.2%	18.7%	3.1%	3.3%
Technology	511210, 518210, 541511, 541512	583	7.8%	20.0%	10.9%	21.6%	9.7%	2.9%	4.1%
Finance and Insurance	52	260		12.4%		8.4%		5.5%	4.9%
Real Estate and Rental and Leasing	53	132	70.9%	11.9%	17.1%	10.6%		68.1%	21.2%
Professional, Scientific, and Technical Services	54	467	32.9%	14.1%	22.9%	19.6%	20.1%	7.9%	4.2%
Consulting	541330, 541612, 541613, 541614, 541618, 541690	112	0.6%	9.3%	13.0%	8.6%	18.5%		2.0%
Management of Companies and Enterprises	55	56		6.7%		12.9%		75.9%	8.2%
Administrative and Support and Waste Management and Remediation Services	56	413	0.1%	16.2%	10.6%	16.6%	14.6%	23.5%	16.0%
Educational Services	61	52		28.3%	19.9%	33.6%	9.3%	19.8%	15.7%
Health Care and Social Assistance	62	260	0.3%	40.4%	10.2%	11.5%		3.8%	8.4%
Arts, Entertainment, and Recreation	71	69				0.1%	4.9%		14.8%
Accommodation and Food Services	72	659	93.2%				7.1%	52.6%	32.6%
Other Services (except Public Administration)	81	492		21.0%	7.4%	5.5%	4.4%	8.1%	23.6%
All Industries	11 - 81	6,329	19.1%	18.4%	18.2%	21.2%	16.3%	15.1%	11.4%

* The total number of observations is the total number of purchase price allocations for each industry. The figure does not necessarily reflect the number of observations for each intangible asset class in the summary information. The count of observations excludes those for noncompetes; there were over 13,000 observations of noncompete lives and values.
The purchase price allocations are organized by sector, according to the North American Industry Classification System. For more information, visit www.census.gov.

Average Intangible Value as a Percentage of Total Intangible Assets, continued										
Industry	Trademarks and Trade Names	Domains	Customer Lists	Customer Contracts	Customer Relationship	Order Backlog	Favorable Contracts	Noncompetes	IPR&D	Goodwill
Agriculture, Forestry, Fishing and Hunting	31.0%				13.5%			3.1%		59.4%
Mining, Quarrying, and Oil and Gas Extraction	3.3%				35.4%		37.3%	9.8%	1.9%	82.1%
Utilities					3.9%		17.3%	0.7%		86.5%
Construction	14.1%		19.9%	7.2%	14.5%	6.2%	28.9%	18.1%		79.5%
Manufacturing	13.5%	1.6%	26.6%	17.5%	25.7%	3.7%	15.9%	16.0%	23.2%	59.8%
Pharmaceuticals	19.1%	0.0%	3.6%	16.7%	25.2%	26.5%	24.1%	8.4%	46.0%	37.1%
Wholesale Trade	18.1%	34.8%	54.1%	35.9%	28.9%	0.7%	29.3%	19.5%	1.6%	66.7%
Retail Trade	13.5%	30.2%	36.5%	23.7%	26.5%		27.0%	24.8%	20.9%	76.2%
Transportation and Warehousing	1.1%	17.9%		21.8%	20.3%	0.7%	30.9%	17.6%		79.6%
Information	4.4%	14.5%	25.4%	12.5%	20.6%	3.0%	23.2%	9.9%	9.5%	61.0%
Software	3.4%	2.9%	20.1%	11.0%	17.4%	3.1%	8.0%	4.6%	8.5%	61.7%
Technology	4.0%	13.6%	24.7%	11.8%	18.4%	2.7%	22.9%	6.4%	10.7%	62.3%
Finance and Insurance	6.9%		50.4%	42.0%	27.5%		28.9%	7.6%	0.0%	70.5%
Real Estate and Rental and Leasing	10.9%	0.4%	10.7%	3.1%	28.5%		11.5%	16.6%	4.2%	75.2%
Professional, Scientific, and Technical Services	8.8%	11.6%	30.7%	23.5%	20.6%	6.6%	15.2%	12.6%	28.0%	69.3%
Consulting	5.5%		23.0%	21.1%	21.3%	13.2%	8.3%	11.9%	1.4%	68.5%
Management of Companies and Enterprises	5.0%		68.9%	12.2%	22.3%	1.6%	10.2%	4.7%	38.5%	62.3%
Administrative and Support and Waste Management and Remediation Services	4.7%	28.0%	24.2%	46.3%	28.6%	3.0%	22.0%	18.6%	21.5%	81.7%
Educational Services		4.4%	30.4%	44.4%	12.6%	17.8%	23.1%	25.5%		69.7%
Health Care and Social Assistance	13.7%		16.7%	52.3%	25.4%	6.3%	28.3%	17.1%	93.8%	81.0%
Arts, Entertainment, and Recreation	25.6%		3.5%				66.7%	26.0%		77.6%
Accommodation and Food Services	26.1%		28.9%	13.8%			32.7%	22.7%		79.9%
Other Services (except Public Administration)	12.2%	33.1%	13.0%	14.0%	11.5%		29.7%	21.8%	35.3%	81.5%
All Industries	10.6%	18.0%	30.9%	21.0%	23.7%	3.9%	24.3%	19.2%	20.4%	69.9%

* The total number of observations is the total number of purchase price allocations for each industry. The figure does not necessarily reflect the number of observations for each intangible asset class in the summary information. The count of observations excludes those for noncompetes; there were over 13,000 observations of noncompete lives and values.
The purchase price allocations are organized by sector, according to the North American Industry Classification System. For more information, visit www.census.gov.

Average Intangible Value as a Percentage of Sold Business Value

Industry	NAICS	Total # of Observations*	Patents	Software	Databases	Technology	Trade Secrets	Trademarks	Trade Names
Agriculture, Forestry, Fishing and Hunting	11	7				46.1%			29.6%
Mining, Quarrying, and Oil and Gas Extraction	21	79		0.4%					3.4%
Utilities	22	25							1.9%
Construction	23	119		7.5%		0.2%		1.6%	15.4%
Manufacturing	31 - 33	1,432	16.5%	8.0%	18.9%	20.1%	9.7%	9.6%	7.3%
Pharmaceuticals	325412	177	33.1%	0.4%		36.7%	7.3%	18.9%	4.3%
Wholesale Trade	42	271	17.1%		45.2%	14.7%	34.4%	24.9%	7.6%
Retail Trade	44 - 45	711		28.6%		9.4%		0.1%	18.4%
Transportation and Warehousing	48 - 49	156		0.4%		3.6%	4.1%	0.7%	6.0%
Information	51	664	6.8%	21.5%	16.3%	22.3%	11.0%	3.1%	4.8%
Software	511210	381	6.8%	22.8%	8.6%	23.0%	21.3%	3.2%	3.6%
Technology	511210, 518210, 541511, 541512	583	9.9%	20.8%	9.7%	23.7%	11.0%	3.0%	4.0%
Finance and Insurance	52	260		7.7%		7.3%		5.9%	4.0%
Real Estate and Rental and Leasing	53	132	68.7%	8.9%	14.9%	10.1%		69.1%	18.8%
Professional, Scientific, and Technical Services	54	467	30.5%	15.6%	19.6%	22.9%	20.5%	7.0%	5.0%
Consulting	541330, 541612, 541613, 541614, 541618, 541690	112	0.7%	6.9%	14.3%	12.4%	23.4%		2.0%
Management of Companies and Enterprises	55	56		7.1%		8.9%		78.4%	6.1%
Administrative and Support and Waste Management and Remediation Services	56	413	0.1%	10.8%	9.2%	15.4%	11.9%	21.8%	12.6%
Educational Services	61	52		20.9%	20.0%	40.6%	9.2%	19.2%	13.5%
Health Care and Social Assistance	62	260	0.2%	38.9%	12.0%	12.2%		3.2%	6.1%
Arts, Entertainment, and Recreation	71	69				0.1%	4.6%		13.2%
Accommodation and Food Services	72	659	20.0%				4.8%	30.7%	15.6%
Other Services (except Public Administration)	81	492		18.7%	8.1%	6.1%	5.6%	7.1%	11.2%
All Industries	11 - 81	6,329	17.8%	17.5%	16.7%	20.1%	13.1%	13.6%	8.4%

* The total number of observations is the total number of purchase price allocations for each industry. The figure does not necessarily reflect the number of observations for each intangible asset class in the summary information. The count of observations excludes those for noncompetes; there were over 13,000 observations of noncompete lives and values.
The purchase price allocations are organized by sector, according to the North American Industry Classification System. For more information, visit www.census.gov.

Average Intangible Value as a Percentage of Sold Business Value, continued										
Industry	Trademarks and Trade Names	Domains	Customer Lists	Customer Contracts	Customer Relationships	Order Backlog	Favorable Contracts	Noncompetes	IPR&D	Goodwill
Agriculture, Forestry, Fishing and Hunting	28.7%				15.6%			2.4%	5.4%	44.4%
Mining, Quarrying, and Oil and Gas Extraction	1.5%				20.2%		50.4%	2.4%	1.6%	29.8%
Utilities					1.2%		42.7%	12.3%		31.4%
Construction	6.2%		8.4%	5.4%	11.9%	4.2%	23.4%	11.9%		52.7%
Manufacturing	10.6%	1.0%	19.3%	13.8%	20.0%	1.9%	11.0%	9.5%	36.7%	95.3%
Pharmaceuticals	17.0%	0.0%	4.1%	14.4%	21.2%	3.9%	20.4%	6.9%	74.5%	36.4%
Wholesale Trade	14.3%	34.7%	41.1%	41.6%	22.6%	0.5%	28.5%	10.3%	1.1%	49.6%
Retail Trade	8.7%	23.6%	25.0%	23.9%	23.5%		18.1%	12.2%	19.1%	46.9%
Transportation and Warehousing	0.8%	8.3%		14.5%	18.5%	0.3%	30.4%	11.6%		50.2%
Information	4.0%	14.7%	23.5%	13.9%	19.2%	3.5%	20.7%	7.7%	9.9%	59.8%
Software	3.5%	2.6%	21.3%	10.8%	17.7%	3.7%	6.6%	4.2%	8.9%	64.3%
Technology	3.9%	13.5%	25.8%	11.9%	17.9%	3.1%	19.1%	6.0%	11.3%	64.3%
Finance and Insurance	7.1%		47.7%	36.0%	25.5%		16.8%	4.4%	0.0%	49.8%
Real Estate and Rental and Leasing	9.3%	0.4%	7.6%	2.7%	18.8%		10.9%	8.5%	3.9%	58.1%
Professional, Scientific, and Technical Services	8.5%	7.5%	32.1%	19.9%	20.7%	5.3%	13.2%	11.0%	39.4%	66.4%
Consulting	6.1%		22.1%	17.8%	23.8%	10.5%	8.1%	8.7%	18.6%	62.0%
Management of Companies and Enterprises	4.0%		54.7%	11.1%	16.7%	1.4%	8.1%	3.2%	49.9%	35.5%
Administrative and Support and Waste Management and Remediation Services	5.0%	12.6%	22.6%	43.1%	24.6%	3.0%	19.1%	13.0%	11.9%	65.4%
Educational Services		4.4%	30.0%	44.4%	13.1%	17.5%	15.7%	10.0%		55.0%
Health Care and Social Assistance	18.6%		15.7%	54.6%	22.5%	5.4%	26.7%	10.0%	93.6%	65.3%
Arts, Entertainment, and Recreation	9.3%		1.5%				35.5%	12.2%		50.4%
Accommodation and Food Services	15.6%		23.8%	7.7%			20.5%	12.4%		43.3%
Other Services (except Public Administration)	9.2%	25.7%	10.1%	22.2%	10.5%		19.0%	12.1%	11.7%	48.0%
All Industries	8.7%	20.4%	25.5%	19.5%	20.2%	2.7%	18.5%	11.1%	30.0%	64.3%

* The total number of observations is the total number of purchase price allocations for each industry. The figure does not necessarily reflect the number of observations for each intangible asset class in the summary information. The count of observations excludes those for noncompetes; there were over 13,000 observations of noncompete lives and values.
The purchase price allocations are organized by sector, according to the North American Industry Classification System. For more information, visit www.census.gov.

Median Intangible Life (years)											
Industry	NAICS	Total # of Observations*	Patents	Software	Databases	Technology	Trade Secrets	Trademarks (when amortized)	Trademarks (# of indefinites)	Trade Names	Trade Names (# of indefinites)
Agriculture, Forestry, Fishing and Hunting	11	7									
Mining, Quarrying, and Oil and Gas Extraction	21	79		5.0 years						40.0 years	1
Utilities	22	25								10.0 years	
Construction	23	119							1	9.5 years	2
Manufacturing	31 - 33	1,432	9.0 years	7.0 years	18.0 years	7.0 years	3.8 years	9.5 years	12	7.0 years	25
Pharmaceuticals	325412	177	10.0 years			11.5 years		13.0 years		5.0 years	
Wholesale Trade	42	271	9.7 years			7.5 years	6.0 years	6.5 years	2	5.5 years	2
Retail Trade	44 - 45	711				4.5 years				5.8 years	3
Transportation and Warehousing	48 - 49	156				15.0 years					1
Information	51	664	5.0 years	5.0 years	7.5 years	5.0 years	3.0 years	4.0 years		5.0 years	5
Software	511210	381	5.0 years	5.5 years	6.0 years	5.0 years	3.0 years	4.5 years		5.0 years	
Technology	511210, 518210, 541511, 541512	583	5.0 years	5.0 years	6.0 years	5.0 years	3.0 years	4.0 years		4.8 years	
Finance and Insurance	52	260		3.0 years		5.0 years		17.5 years		5.0 years	4
Real Estate and Rental and Leasing	53	132	6.5 years	3.0 years	6.0 years	6.0 years		5.0 years	2	13.0 years	
Professional, Scientific, and Technical Services	54	467	9.5 years	5.0 years	8.0 years	6.7 years	5.5 years	11.0 years	1	3.0 years	2
Consulting	541330, 541612, 541613, 541614, 541618, 541690	112		6.0 years	10.0 years	5.0 years	6.0 years			4.0 years	
Management of Companies and Enterprises	55	56		5.0 years		20.0 years				17.5 years	
Administrative and Support and Waste Management and Remediation Services	56	413		4.5 years	15.0 years	5.5 years	35.0 years	15.0 years	1	7.0 years	5
Educational Services	61	52					5.0 years		1	15.0 years	1
Health Care and Social Assistance	62	260	5.0 years			7.0 years		8.0 years	1	5.0 years	1
Arts, Entertainment, and Recreation	71	69									
Accommodation and Food Services	72	659							1		
Other Services (except Public Administration)	81	492			10.0 years	3.3 years	10.0 years	15.0 years		10.0 years	1
All Industries	11 - 81	6,329	7.0 years	5.0 years	10.0 years	6.0 years	5.0 years	7.0 years	22	5.0 years	53

* The total number of observations is the total number of purchase price allocations for each industry. The figure does not necessarily reflect the number of observations for each intangible asset class in the summary information. The count of observations excludes those for noncompetes; there were over 13,000 observations of noncompete lives and values.
The purchase price allocations are organized by sector, according to the North American Industry Classification System. For more information, visit www.census.gov.

Median Intangible Life (years), continued												
Industry	Trademarks and Trade Names	Trademarks and Trade Names (# of indefinites)	Domains	Customer Lists	Customer Contracts	Customer Relationships	Order Backlog	Favorable Contracts	Noncompetes	IPR&D (when amortized)	IPR&D (# of indefinites)	IPR&D (# of expensed)
Agriculture, Forestry, Fishing and Hunting									5.0 years			
Mining, Quarrying, and Oil and Gas Extraction						15.0 years		3.0 years	5.0 years			
Utilities						11.8 years		1.5 years	5.0 years			
Construction					3.0 years	10.0 years	5.1 years	15.5 years	5.0 years			
Manufacturing	10.0 years	10		11.3 years	7.0 years	10.0 years	1.0 years	5.5 years	5.0 years	7.3 years	6	6
Pharmaceuticals	10.2 years				12.0 years	12.0 years	1.5 years	10.0 years	3.0 years			
Wholesale Trade		1		17.0 years	4.0 years	10.0 years	0.3 years	6.0 years	5.0 years			
Retail Trade	3.2 years			4.0 years	15.0 years	9.5 years		17.9 years	5.0 years			
Transportation and Warehousing						13.5 years	0.1 years	16.0 years	5.0 years			
Information	10.0 years	2	6.5 years	9.0 years	7.0 years	7.0 years	2.0 years	6.0 years	3.0 years	7.0 years	1	4
Software	10.0 years		3.0 years	10.0 years	7.0 years	7.0 years	2.0 years	5.0 years	3.0 years	7.0 years		
Technology	9.0 years		3.0 years	16.0 years	6.0 years	7.5 years	1.5 years	5.0 years	3.0 years	7.0 years		
Finance and Insurance	5.0 years	1		10.8 years	10.0 years	12.0 years		8.3 years	3.0 years		1	
Real Estate and Rental and Leasing	5.0 years	2			1.0 years	8.0 years		18.0 years	5.0 years			
Professional, Scientific, and Technical Services	7.5 years	2		7.0 years	4.0 years	10.0 years	1.0 years	5.5 years	5.0 years		1	
Consulting	10.0 years			7.0 years	1.5 years	10.0 years	2.1 years	9.0 years	4.0 years			
Management of Companies and Enterprises				18.0 years	8.0 years	15.0 years	3.0 years	23.0 years	2.0 years			
Administrative and Support and Waste Management and Remediation Services	23.3 years	2	19.0 years	3.5 years	5.5 years	12.0 years	5.4 years	30.0 years	5.0 years			1
Educational Services						3.0 years			3.0 years			
Health Care and Social Assistance	10.0 years					10.0 years	3.0 years	10.5 years	3.0 years			
Arts, Entertainment, and Recreation									5.0 years			
Accommodation and Food Services									5.0 years			
Other Services (except Public Administration)	4.0 years			5.0 years	5.0 years	5.0 years		22.5 years	5.0 years			
All Industries	8.5 years	20	10.0 years	10.0 years	6.0 years	9.5 years	1.0 years	6.8 years	5.0 years	7.0 years	9	11

* The total number of observations is the total number of purchase price allocations for each industry. The figure does not necessarily reflect the number of observations for each intangible asset class in the summary information. The count of observations excludes those for noncompetes; there were over 13,000 observations of noncompete lives and values.
The purchase price allocations are organized by sector, according to the North American Industry Classification System. For more information, visit www.census.gov.

Median Intangible Value as a Percentage of Identifiable Intangible Assets

Industry	NAICS	Total # of Observations*	Patents	Software	Databases	Technology	Trade Secrets	Trademarks	Trade Names
Agriculture, Forestry, Fishing and Hunting	11	7				63.1%			64.4%
Mining, Quarrying, and Oil and Gas Extraction	21	79		1.4%					18.5%
Utilities	22	25							6.0%
Construction	23	119		100.0%		1.1%		12.7%	43.6%
Manufacturing	31 - 33	1,432	20.7%	3.8%	50.3%	45.4%	23.2%	10.3%	11.8%
Pharmaceuticals	325412	177	45.7%	1.0%		47.4%	47.6%	23.4%	3.9%
Wholesale Trade	42	271	27.2%		100.0%	15.0%	55.0%	36.0%	12.7%
Retail Trade	44 - 45	711		100.0%		16.1%		8.3%	50.0%
Transportation and Warehousing	48 - 49	156		16.0%		22.9%	100.0%	7.1%	34.6%
Information	51	664	8.4%	29.6%	31.0%	46.3%	14.4%	5.4%	5.2%
Software	511210	381	11.4%	30.4%	11.0%	48.4%	27.4%	3.5%	3.6%
Technology	511210, 518210, 541511, 541512	583	11.0%	28.0%	15.4%	48.4%	14.4%	3.5%	4.5%
Finance and Insurance	52	260		15.1%		14.3%		10.7%	5.8%
Real Estate and Rental and Leasing	53	132	100.0%	4.2%	30.2%	26.6%		96.1%	46.0%
Professional, Scientific, and Technical Services	54	467	19.1%	25.5%	46.6%	43.4%	30.9%	9.0%	6.7%
Consulting	541330, 541612, 541613, 541614, 541618, 541690	112	2.3%	11.1%	46.6%	21.8%	38.3%		3.8%
Management of Companies and Enterprises	55	56		21.6%		21.9%		91.5%	12.6%
Administrative and Support and Waste Management and Remediation Services	56	413	0.2%	11.8%	20.0%	20.2%	24.8%	36.0%	21.5%
Educational Services	61	52		14.2%	38.5%	61.8%	21.5%	85.0%	40.6%
Health Care and Social Assistance	62	260	1.3%	30.4%	15.9%	21.0%		11.4%	12.6%
Arts, Entertainment, and Recreation	71	69				0.1%	5.1%		25.3%
Accommodation and Food Services	72	659	93.2%				100.0%	86.9%	45.2%
Other Services (except Public Administration)	81	492		90.6%	19.7%	15.5%	17.4%	14.6%	41.0%
All Industries	11 - 81	6,329	18.6%	25.3%	36.8%	43.5%	26.1%	10.9%	14.1%

* The total number of observations is the total number of purchase price allocations for each industry. The figure does not necessarily reflect the number of observations for each intangible asset class in the summary information. The count of observations excludes those for noncompetes; there were over 13,000 observations of noncompete lives and values.
The purchase price allocations are organized by sector, according to the North American Industry Classification System. For more information, visit www.census.gov.

Median Intangible Value as a Percentage of Identifiable Intangible Assets, continued									
Industry	Trademarks and Trade Names	Domains	Customer Lists	Customer Contracts	Customer Relationships	Order Backlog	Favorable Contracts	Noncompetes	IPR&D
Agriculture, Forestry, Fishing and Hunting	41.5%				17.2%			3.0%	
Mining, Quarrying, and Oil and Gas Extraction	5.7%				75.5%		5.5%	18.9%	5.0%
Utilities					35.9%		33.3%		
Construction	54.3%		29.9%	32.2%	28.6%	15.0%	25.4%	34.3%	
Manufacturing	14.8%	0.6%	73.5%	25.0%	40.4%	2.6%	10.8%	4.9%	21.3%
Pharmaceuticals	34.3%	0.0%	7.8%	25.0%	34.9%	26.5%	24.5%	9.3%	58.1%
Wholesale Trade	23.4%	44.9%	66.7%	85.1%	75.2%	1.0%	28.1%	10.0%	3.1%
Retail Trade	52.8%	27.3%	41.7%	17.5%	46.1%		40.0%	39.8%	45.5%
Transportation and Warehousing	3.5%	100.0%		77.5%	72.5%	2.5%	20.6%	16.3%	
Information	6.2%	19.1%	39.1%	27.8%	46.0%	4.6%	12.5%	4.0%	10.0%
Software	4.7%	6.4%	27.0%	23.4%	42.1%	5.1%	8.7%	3.9%	10.2%
Technology	5.0%	6.4%	49.0%	26.3%	42.8%	4.6%	9.1%	3.7%	11.5%
Finance and Insurance	9.7%		100.0%	83.4%	63.1%		7.3%	4.9%	0.0%
Real Estate and Rental and Leasing	17.2%	0.5%	66.7%	5.7%	59.1%		5.2%	7.8%	7.0%
Professional, Scientific, and Technical Services	5.8%	12.0%	52.4%	54.1%	62.5%	4.9%	8.4%	5.0%	32.4%
Consulting	6.3%		38.4%	37.6%	69.1%	11.6%	10.9%	16.0%	4.6%
Management of Companies and Enterprises	5.2%		94.6%	52.0%	57.5%	2.7%	42.3%	8.8%	45.6%
Administrative and Support and Waste Management and Remediation Services	7.3%	50.2%	88.1%	94.9%	68.7%	8.3%	34.7%	17.9%	24.8%
Educational Services		4.7%	20.9%	46.5%	34.5%	21.7%	27.1%	12.1%	
Health Care and Social Assistance	25.9%		67.6%	63.8%	67.2%	32.8%	37.6%	6.0%	100.0%
Arts, Entertainment, and Recreation	71.4%		27.3%					66.7%	
Accommodation and Food Services	100.0%		70.0%	43.9%			37.1%	40.5%	
Other Services (except Public Administration)	6.3%	88.2%	41.7%	24.6%	36.3%		35.0%	33.6%	100.0%
All Industries	11.2%	21.7%	51.2%	32.3%	46.7%	3.6%	17.7%	12.1%	17.7%

* The total number of observations is the total number of purchase price allocations for each industry. The figure does not necessarily reflect the number of observations for each intangible asset class in the summary information. The count of observations excludes those for noncompetes; there were over 13,000 observations of noncompete lives and values.
The purchase price allocations are organized by sector, according to the North American Industry Classification System. For more information, visit www.census.gov.

Median Intangible Value as a Percentage of Total Intangible Assets

Industry	NAICS	Total # of Observations*	Patents	Software	Databases	Technology	Trade Secrets	Trademarks	Trade Names
Agriculture, Forestry, Fishing and Hunting	11	7				47.3%			55.9%
Mining, Quarrying, and Oil and Gas Extraction	21	79		0.5%					6.6%
Utilities	22	25							6.0%
Construction	23	119		8.4%		0.5%		3.7%	18.6%
Manufacturing	31 - 33	1,432	7.3%	2.0%	18.8%	19.1%	7.7%	5.2%	5.6%
Pharmaceuticals	325412	177	31.7%	0.4%		26.4%	17.3%	12.1%	2.4%
Wholesale Trade	42	271	10.1%		86.4%	7.4%	50.9%	25.2%	6.5%
Retail Trade	44 - 45	711		29.8%		4.2%		0.1%	23.8%
Transportation and Warehousing	48 - 49	156		0.6%		7.0%	5.8%	0.5%	7.8%
Information	51	664	5.0%	12.6%	7.0%	16.2%	9.7%	1.7%	1.9%
Software	511210	381	5.2%	13.4%	3.5%	16.4%	18.7%	2.0%	1.6%
Technology	511210, 518210, 541511, 541512	583	5.0%	11.7%	4.3%	16.5%	9.7%	1.7%	1.6%
Finance and Insurance	52	260		6.9%		3.7%		4.5%	2.1%
Real Estate and Rental and Leasing	53	132	73.5%	2.3%	6.5%	9.8%		87.6%	17.3%
Professional, Scientific, and Technical Services	54	467	5.8%	7.2%	13.0%	14.2%	22.4%	3.2%	1.6%
Consulting	541330, 541612, 541613, 541614, 541618, 541690	112	0.6%	3.3%	13.0%	7.3%	18.5%		1.3%
Management of Companies and Enterprises	55	56		6.7%		10.8%		75.9%	7.0%
Administrative and Support and Waste Management and Remediation Services	56	413	0.1%	9.4%	10.4%	10.4%	14.6%	29.4%	11.7%
Educational Services	61	52		5.7%	19.9%	33.6%	9.3%	19.8%	15.7%
Health Care and Social Assistance	62	260	0.3%	18.1%	10.2%	3.1%		2.7%	6.3%
Arts, Entertainment, and Recreation	71	69				0.1%	4.9%		14.8%
Accommodation and Food Services	72	659	93.2%				7.1%	52.6%	25.0%
Other Services (except Public Administration)	81	492		21.0%	7.4%	5.5%	4.4%	8.1%	21.5%
All Industries	11 - 81	6,329	7.1%	9.1%	9.1%	16.0%	11.8%	4.6%	6.0%

* The total number of observations is the total number of purchase price allocations for each industry. The figure does not necessarily reflect the number of observations for each intangible asset class in the summary information. The count of observations excludes those for noncompetes; there were over 13,000 observations of noncompete lives and values.
The purchase price allocations are organized by sector, according to the North American Industry Classification System. For more information, visit www.census.gov.

Median Intangible Value as a Percentage of Total Intangible Assets, continued

Industry	Trademarks and Trade Names	Domains	Customer Lists	Customer Contracts	Customer Relationship	Order Backlog	Favorable Contracts	Noncompetes	IPR&D	Goodwill
Agriculture, Forestry, Fishing and Hunting	31.0%				12.9%			3.1%		60.7%
Mining, Quarrying, and Oil and Gas Extraction	3.3%				34.2%		37.3%	9.8%	1.9%	100.0%
Utilities					3.9%		17.3%	0.7%		93.2%
Construction	14.1%		14.8%	2.7%	9.6%	6.2%	20.5%	11.2%		92.6%
Manufacturing	6.2%	0.6%	20.0%	12.8%	18.3%	1.3%	7.2%	5.3%	10.0%	59.2%
Pharmaceuticals	16.8%	0.0%	3.6%	16.5%	16.9%	26.5%	22.0%	5.7%	38.9%	29.9%
Wholesale Trade	18.1%	32.1%	48.5%	36.1%	27.6%	0.3%	24.5%	9.9%	1.6%	70.8%
Retail Trade	12.4%	13.8%	22.7%	6.2%	17.7%		18.2%	17.3%	20.9%	87.3%
Transportation and Warehousing	1.1%	17.9%		25.3%	19.7%	0.7%	21.9%	9.8%		94.2%
Information	2.4%	2.8%	12.9%	10.1%	16.1%	1.9%	13.5%	2.8%	4.5%	62.7%
Software	2.0%	2.6%	10.8%	7.9%	14.3%	1.5%	3.7%	1.5%	4.3%	64.1%
Technology	2.3%	2.6%	17.0%	9.9%	14.8%	1.6%	11.4%	1.6%	4.3%	64.1%
Finance and Insurance	6.1%		56.7%	40.5%	21.5%		16.8%	1.8%	0.0%	76.3%
Real Estate and Rental and Leasing	8.7%	0.4%	12.7%	3.1%	29.6%		6.0%	6.3%	4.2%	90.3%
Professional, Scientific, and Technical Services	2.5%	11.6%	25.1%	17.1%	16.8%	1.7%	6.1%	5.5%	10.8%	73.0%
Consulting	2.7%		23.2%	8.8%	18.4%	4.7%	4.9%	4.9%	1.2%	70.4%
Management of Companies and Enterprises	2.3%		68.9%	11.9%	21.2%	1.6%	5.6%	5.7%	38.5%	72.5%
Administrative and Support and Waste Management and Remediation Services	3.5%	28.0%	18.7%	54.0%	25.7%	3.3%	17.3%	10.0%	21.5%	96.9%
Educational Services		4.4%	20.0%	44.4%	12.2%	17.8%	19.4%	19.0%		67.8%
Health Care and Social Assistance	13.7%		16.7%	52.3%	22.1%	6.3%	20.6%	9.8%	93.8%	92.2%
Arts, Entertainment, and Recreation	25.6%		3.5%				66.7%	20.9%		85.4%
Accommodation and Food Services	16.3%		28.9%	13.8%			21.6%	15.6%		95.6%
Other Services (except Public Administration)	2.2%	39.6%	8.7%	14.0%	12.6%		25.7%	13.5%	35.3%	96.9%
All Industries	5.2%	4.3%	20.0%	12.9%	18.2%	1.6%	14.9%	10.0%	7.3%	73.3%

* The total number of observations is the total number of purchase price allocations for each industry. The figure does not necessarily reflect the number of observations for each intangible asset class in the summary information. The count of observations excludes those for noncompetes; there were over 13,000 observations of noncompete lives and values.
The purchase price allocations are organized by sector, according to the North American Industry Classification System. For more information, visit www.census.gov.

Median Intangible Value as a Percentage of Sold Business Value									
Industry	NAICS	Total # of Observations*	Patents	Software	Databases	Technology	Trade Secrets	Trademarks	Trade Names
Agriculture, Forestry, Fishing and Hunting	11	7				46.1%			29.6%
Mining, Quarrying, and Oil and Gas Extraction	21	79		0.4%					3.4%
Utilities	22	25							1.9%
Construction	23	119		7.5%		0.2%		1.6%	16.6%
Manufacturing	31 - 33	1,432	6.6%	1.7%	18.9%	14.7%	4.2%	3.3%	4.4%
Pharmaceuticals	325412	177	27.7%	0.4%		25.5%	3.4%	10.9%	2.2%
Wholesale Trade	42	271	10.6%		45.2%	7.8%	35.3%	23.5%	4.2%
Retail Trade	44 - 45	711		21.5%		8.5%		0.1%	14.5%
Transportation and Warehousing	48 - 49	156		0.4%		3.6%	4.1%	0.3%	2.6%
Information	51	664	5.6%	12.0%	6.8%	15.9%	11.0%	1.7%	1.8%
Software	511210	381	5.3%	13.5%	3.6%	16.2%	21.3%	2.3%	1.5%
Technology	511210, 518210, 541511, 541512	583	4.9%	10.9%	3.6%	16.8%	11.0%	2.1%	1.6%
Finance and Insurance	52	260		7.1%		3.0%		4.9%	1.9%
Real Estate and Rental and Leasing	53	132	83.3%	2.0%	5.9%	9.3%		88.0%	11.4%
Professional, Scientific, and Technical Services	54	467	4.9%	7.4%	14.3%	13.9%	14.7%	2.9%	1.4%
Consulting	541330, 541612, 541613, 541614, 541618, 541690	112	0.7%	2.8%	14.3%	7.0%	23.4%		1.4%
Management of Companies and Enterprises	55	56		7.1%		9.2%		78.4%	4.7%
Administrative and Support and Waste Management and Remediation Services	56	413	0.1%	10.3%	7.0%	10.0%	11.9%	23.5%	8.5%
Educational Services	61	52		5.4%	20.0%	40.6%	9.2%	19.2%	13.5%
Health Care and Social Assistance	62	260	0.2%	25.3%	12.0%	3.3%		2.6%	5.6%
Arts, Entertainment, and Recreation	71	69				0.1%	4.6%		13.2%
Accommodation and Food Services	72	659	20.0%				4.8%	30.7%	16.3%
Other Services (except Public Administration)	81	492		18.7%	8.1%	6.1%	5.6%	7.1%	6.1%
All Industries	11 - 81	6,329	6.6%	8.1%	10.5%	13.8%	6.9%	3.7%	4.4%

* The total number of observations is the total number of purchase price allocations for each industry. The figure does not necessarily reflect the number of observations for each intangible asset class in the summary information. The count of observations excludes those for noncompetes; there were over 13,000 observations of noncompete lives and values.
The purchase price allocations are organized by sector, according to the North American Industry Classification System. For more information, visit www.census.gov.

Median Intangible Value as a Percentage of Sold Business Value, continued										
Industry	Trademarks and Trade Names	Domains	Customer Lists	Customer Contracts	Customer Relationships	Order Backlog	Favorable Contracts	Noncompetes	IPR&D	Goodwill
Agriculture, Forestry, Fishing and Hunting	28.7%				17.7%			2.5%	5.4%	24.4%
Mining, Quarrying, and Oil and Gas Extraction	1.5%				19.4%		67.8%	1.9%	1.6%	29.7%
Utilities					1.2%		41.8%	0.4%		30.5%
Construction	6.2%		7.0%	2.3%	4.8%	4.2%	17.3%	7.5%		57.1%
Manufacturing	5.2%	0.9%	10.6%	10.0%	13.2%	1.0%	5.4%	3.8%	7.5%	44.4%
Pharmaceuticals	14.6%	0.0%	4.1%	14.8%	10.8%	3.9%	15.4%	5.6%	37.5%	32.1%
Wholesale Trade	18.1%	53.3%	33.1%	38.9%	23.8%	0.3%	19.6%	5.5%	1.1%	45.1%
Retail Trade	6.3%	8.0%	11.3%	5.6%	13.8%		8.0%	8.2%	19.1%	45.3%
Transportation and Warehousing	0.8%	8.3%		19.7%	6.3%	0.3%	13.8%	6.7%		47.3%
Information	2.4%	2.6%	10.6%	10.1%	15.4%	1.9%	10.3%	2.9%	4.1%	60.7%
Software	1.9%	2.0%	10.6%	7.5%	13.7%	1.4%	3.9%	1.3%	4.1%	65.6%
Technology	2.0%	2.0%	13.6%	8.3%	14.6%	1.7%	9.3%	1.9%	4.2%	63.6%
Finance and Insurance	7.4%		56.7%	39.4%	15.9%		4.5%	1.4%	0.0%	47.5%
Real Estate and Rental and Leasing	7.4%	0.4%	5.4%	2.7%	20.7%		3.8%	3.9%	3.9%	58.9%
Professional, Scientific, and Technical Services	2.3%	7.5%	25.4%	11.1%	15.7%	1.7%	5.2%	4.2%	12.1%	66.5%
Consulting	2.5%		19.2%	8.8%	16.0%	4.0%	4.3%	4.5%	2.1%	65.9%
Management of Companies and Enterprises	2.2%		54.7%	12.0%	17.1%	1.4%	2.4%	3.4%	49.9%	30.0%
Administrative and Support and Waste Management and Remediation Services	3.1%	12.6%	17.7%	40.3%	21.6%	4.1%	16.2%	8.3%	11.9%	68.1%
Educational Services		4.4%	20.0%	44.4%	11.1%	17.5%	18.1%	8.0%		56.6%
Health Care and Social Assistance	18.6%		15.7%	54.6%	17.2%	5.4%	10.8%	6.6%	93.6%	68.2%
Arts, Entertainment, and Recreation	9.3%		1.5%				35.5%	7.0%		53.3%
Accommodation and Food Services	7.6%		23.8%	7.7%			15.4%	8.1%		39.2%
Other Services (except Public Administration)	2.2%	31.3%	7.5%	22.2%	11.3%		17.4%	7.1%	11.7%	45.5%
All Industries	4.2%	4.1%	13.9%	10.6%	14.8%	1.3%	10.2%	5.9%	5.9%	50.6%

* The total number of observations is the total number of purchase price allocations for each industry. The figure does not necessarily reflect the number of observations for each intangible asset class in the summary information. The count of observations excludes those for noncompetes; there were over 13,000 observations of noncompete lives and values.
The purchase price allocations are organized by sector, according to the North American Industry Classification System. For more information, visit www.census.gov.

www.ingramcontent.com/pod-product-compliance
Ingram Content Group UK Ltd.
Pitfield, Milton Keynes, MK11 3LW, UK
UKHW051508290926
15471UKWH00008B/1490

9 781621 500568